D1628690

COMPLETE PRAYERS
FOR TEENAGERS

compiled by

Nick Aiken

Marshall Pickering
An Imprint of HarperCollins*Publishers*

Marshall Pickering is an Imprint of
HarperCollins*Religious*
Part of HarperCollins*Publishers*
77–85 Fulham Palace Road, London W6 8JB

Prayers for Teenagers first published in Great Britain
in 1989 by Marshall Morgan and Scott,
forerunner of Marshall Pickering

More Prayers for Teenagers first published in Great Britain
in 1993 by Marshall Pickering

Copyright © 1989, 1993 Nick Aiken

1 3 5 7 9 10 8 6 4 2

Nick Aiken asserts the moral right to be
identified as the compiler of this work

A catalogue record for this book is
available from the British Library

ISBN 0 551 03151 4

Printed and bound in Great Britain by
Caledonian International Book Manufacturing Ltd, Glasgow

Foreword

THESE ARE honest prayers written by teenagers for teenagers. In fact, this book is a combination of two very successful books which have sold in their thousands, *Prayers for Teenagers* and *More Prayers for Teenagers*. Hundreds of young people throughout the country have contributed to this book, which covers a complete range of issues which concern teenagers today. All royalties are donated to the Prince's Trust.

This book is great as a gift for someone's birthday or confirmation. It can be used for personal prayer or in a church, at the youth group or in a school assembly. I have many favourite prayers from this book – find out which one is yours!

Nick Aiken

Contents

Contents

Acknowledgements

Prayers for Teenagers

I HAVE a vast number of people to thank who have contributed towards this book of prayers for teenagers. I received prayers from young people all over the country, though mainly from teenagers who are members of youth groups from the Guildford Diocese. I would like to thank Martin Hook, Anna Matthews, Melissa Sherwood, Katherine Wilson, Marion Hore, Edward Fraser, Katy Watkins, Helen Askew, David Butcher, Ben Taylor, Anna-Marie Rotheisen, Richard Markwick, Andrew Vincent, Zimba Moore, Gillian Elsmore, Richard Huxley, Julie Guyer, Tanya Lancaster, Natasha Fraser, Julie Arthur, Tammy Harris, Esther Rich, Marguerite Devanney, Nicola Woodgate, Rachel Curtis, Nikki King, Charlie Olsen, Alex Barlow, Jane Curtis, Katherine White, Suzanne Green, Guy Travers, Sally Hawkins, Sophia Moore,

Debbie Clark, Vicky Fraser, Emma King, Nick Hyde, Matthew Thomas, Lucy Bouch, Tracy Godwin, Jane Hanson, Katy Watkins, Ned Palfrey, Susanna Martin, Gabrielle Allnutt, Julia Dignan, Jo Cotton, Lucie Brailsford, Karen Willson, Paul Humphrey, Steven Knight, Vicky Searchfield, Colin McCoy, Julia Stevens, Simon Martin, Karen Taylor, Suzanna Earle, Sarah McLogan, Jo Teasdale, Nikki Simmonds, Louise Aiken, Alison Buller, Rachel Fellingham, Katherine Short, Claire Revel, Lucinda Thurnhurst, Kirsty Hook, Jo Coward, Sara Wilson, Sarah Warne, Stephanie Edwards, Gavin Brainbridge, Zoe Smale, Sammie Harvey, David Barber, Lucy Baines, Jill Bowdery, Emma Matthews, Tim Rose, Beverley Polington, Stephen Willson, Claire Morse, Sarah Goodson, Cathy Porter and many whose prayers are included in this book but whose name I don't know.

I hope as you read and use the prayers in this book you will find them of help and an inspiration.

I would also like to thank Ruth Drury, Tammy Harris, Claire Morse, Suzanna Martin, Robert Tobias, Lisa Stubbing, Emma-Jane Ericson, Sonya McAnulla, Stephen McAnulla, Gillian Elsmore, Rachel Curtis, Jane Curtis, Rosie Goddard, Jonathan Beasley, Nick

Vincent, Alex Griffin, Natasha Fraser, Tracy Crow, Richard Markwick, Frances Wood, Ned Palfrey and Tanya Lancaster who helped me in choosing the prayers and compiling the book. Their assistance was of immense value and to them I am very grateful.

To my colleagues in the Education Department at Diocesan House I am grateful for all their help and support. In particular I would like to thank Anne Plunkett who laboured in typing the manuscript and who is a patient and excellent secretary.

As you may know all the royalties from this book will go to the work of the Prince's Trust. The Trust does such valuable and important work among young people in Britain today. It is a privilege to be involved in its work and I hope that the money the book earns will give a lot of valuable help to young people throughout the country.

Finally, may I stress that all the prayers in this book are basically unedited: they are an expression of what the teenagers felt and the way they wanted to articulate it.

More Prayers for Teenagers

I HAVE a great many people to thank who have helped in compiling this book of prayers. Firstly over a thousand young people from all over the country but particularly in the Guildford Diocese who sent me their prayers. Thank you for taking the trouble. The vast majority have been printed in the manner and style in which they were written so as you can see there has been no heavy editing.

I also need to thank a small group of teenagers who during a weekend away went through all the prayers and selected the ones they wanted to see printed. So thanks to Matthew Hastings, Hannah James, Tammy and James Wakefield, Hannah Judson, Carolyn Butcher, Mark Webster, Simon Collier, Marc Smith, Susan Everest, Magnus Smith, Helen Baker, Nicholas Tobias, Nick Vincent, Rachel Curtis, Matthew Beasley and Charlotte Bateson.

Thanks also to those whose prayers are printed in this book. They are Nick Clover, Angela Hoffman, James Wakefield, Nicola Watson, Nick Wilsdon, Natasha Frazer, Tina Hutchinson, Laura Holliday, Ben Moulden, Lindsay Blundell, Matthew Thomas, Nicola

Henderson, Elizabeth Mitchell, Hannah James, Julie Stephens, David Paradise, Ben Cope, James Read, Dawn Hayden, Russell Nixon, Richard Moore, Lisa Smith, Sarah Tregaskes, Harvey Wade, Helen Pool, Helen Kay, Stuart Sutherland, Ross Manton, Adele Nichols, Sarah Erle, Catherine Corrigan, Kevin Painting, Liz White, Sophie Bolland, Paul Wheeler, Alison Smith, Kathryn Brooks, Claire Andrews, Alex Brading, Mike Scott, Lorna Belmore, Steve McAnnulla, Lorraine Simmonds, Katherine Seagar, Mark Webster, Susan Everest, Lucy Matthews, Louise Abson, Guy Moss, Caroline Martin, Davina Lassiter, Judith Winborn, Jenny Coles, Helen Morton, Will Phillips, Kathryn Loader, Catherine Fielder, Emma Wareham, Eleanor Wareham, Vicky Slater, Debbie Mayne, Natalie Jones, Suzanne Sanger, Rebecca Dane, Lorraine Knowles, David Allison, Mark Day, Michelle Savage, Steven James, Charlotte Curtis, Emma Hancock, David Beasley, Abby Cronin, Andrea Marley, Lynda Biddlecombe, Alison Smith, Imogen Rowling, Nicki Simmonds, Tammy Harris, Julie Guyer, Jo Cotton, Catherine Short, Amber Murrell, Kerry Thomas, Brian Colston, Rowland Johnson, Thomas Coward, Natasha Wilson, Elizabeth Steynor, Helen Sloan, Joanna Teasdale, Miriam Jefferys, Rebecca Thompson, Jonathan Beasley, Mark Auckland, Daryl Chapman, Tasha Reddin, Jemma Richards, Vicky Leeman, Alice Palmer, Cathy Porter, Cecilia Mearing-Smith, Helen Burges, Eleanor

Swanson, Russell Nixon, Gayle Rix, Bonnie Clarke and Robert Tobias.

Also thanks to the many other young people whose prayers are printed in this book but who did not put their name to them.

Nick Aiken

PRAYERS
FOR TEENAGERS

To Mum and Dad, Sharon
and Louise,
with much love and thanks

1

Some helpful thoughts on how to pray

PRAYER IS WONDERFUL. It allows God to look into us and see us. Women and men down the centuries have discovered that prayer is in fact a very crucial part of life. Without prayer, life can be very hard and dry. But when we allow God to look into us and when we look at him then something very powerful happens. It brings us back to life. It puts us in touch with God. So what is prayer all about?

Well let's start with God. It is God who is our Father in heaven. It is he who cares about us — loves us and because he has made us his children it is only right that we should come to him with our thanks and gratitude and requests. After all he created us.

So what does God want us to do — well, to love and worship him. To commit our lives to him and to show that we love him by our words and actions. He wants to change our lives — to make them better. He

1

wants us to be strong and courageous so that what we do we do out of love and trust.

You see prayer brings us right into the presence of God. It is like opening a door which allows you to go inside to this vast throne room where God is present as King and Ruler. Prayer is a privilege. No one would think about bursting into God's presence – rather you should come in gently and reverently remembering who it is you are talking to. Do you remember when Jesus taught the disciples the Lord's Prayer he said we should begin by saying 'Our Father who art in heaven, hallowed be your name...' In other words God reigns in heaven as Lord and Ruler and his name is to be honoured and revered. But the wonderful thing is that this great and mighty king actually allows us to come into his presence – he invites us in, to come and sit with him and talk and discuss all that concerns and worries us – actually like a friend.

Well what should we talk to him about. Of course about our concerns, but much more than that. We should talk about him and what he has done for us. There are plenty of things we can thank him for – our life, food, health, parents, friends, family, a job. There will always be something positive, something good that we can find that we should say thank you for. In fact if you really think about it there will be a multitude of things – both great and small that it is worth saying thank you for. You don't have to get carried away with it but just show and express your gratitude.

Have you ever been to a pop concert? Most of you I guess will say yes, and if you have not been then you probably hope to go one day. They are very noisy affairs with lots of energy, lights and enthusiasm. You can almost see the sound of music hit the roof and bounce off. Well that's a little like heaven: the angels' praise and worship hits the roof.

God wants us to worship him sometimes quietly and reverently but sometimes with a loud voice as well. Sometimes we may feel we want to shout his praises from the rooftops, thanking him for all he has done. If you feel that way at times don't ever think it's inappropriate because Psalm 47 says:

> Clap your hands, all peoples!
> Shout to God with loud songs of joy
> For the Lord, the Most High, is terrible,
> a great King over all the earth.

I don't think that heaven is quiet all of the time. In fact I'm sure it is a pretty noisy and exciting place.

It is terribly important that we should express our gratitude and thanks to God because there is nothing worse than someone who does not show their gratitude and say thank you. It is very rude. You can probably remember the times you have hurt when someone has not bothered to show their appreciation. Well you can imagine what God feels – so it's important to say thanks.

So what should we do next? Well, pray for others. Pray for your Mum. Pray that God may bless her. If she has had a hard time ask that she may be given strength and courage to do her work. Try and make life easier for her by offering some practical help. Make your bed. Tidy your room. Ease the hassle that makes things difficult at times.

Pray for your Dad. Maybe things have been difficult at work with various pressures. Being out of work is worse. Work can involve a lot of stress because of all the various responsibilities involved. Pray for Dad. Pray that your relationship with him may improve and grow stronger. Dads as well as Mums are very special so they deserve our prayers. You may not get on very well with your parents at times and things may be pretty bad at home. But prayer can help. It can help you see your parents in a better light. It can help you understand what they feel. It is actually not easy being a parent. It's hard work and sometimes *you* don't make it any easier. So show your love and care and ask God to bless your family.

Then what about your friends and their ups and downs? It's great to have friends. In fact friends are absolutely crucial. Just think where you would be without them – sometimes you might think better off! Friends can irritate you and get you down but actually we all know that we need them. So pray for them. Be kind to them and try to show them your love and care.

Prayer is so important because it strengthens our relationships with our friends. It shows that we are thinking of them and wish that only good shall come their way. Prayer can make a relationship special and it's great to be able to pray for our friends because of the strength and help it can give them.

Prayer is also concerned with saying sorry. Sometimes we do not tell the truth. We are unkind and selfish to others. Well we cannot come into God's presence as if nothing has happened; rather we must ask God to forgive us. It might be an idea to stop for a few moments during your prayers and just recall the things that you know you've done wrong. Maybe you were bad tempered with someone or bitchy behind their backs saying something that was cruel. Maybe your thoughts were filled with sexual ideas which you know were not good. The great thing is that we need not walk around feeling guilty about what we have done wrong because when we ask God to forgive us – he does! He forgives and forgets. No matter what we have done or how bad it is he will forgive us and because he forgives us he wants us to forgive others.

Prayer is also about being quiet at times. Things may be noisy at home so where do you go to be quiet? Well, of course, there is always your bedroom if you are lucky to have one of your own. But sometimes going off for a walk gives the opportunity of being alone to think and pray. In fact Jesus at times just couldn't cope with the vast crowds that followed him and chased after him so he used to go up into the mountains to pray and listen to God.

There may not be too many mountains round where you live but there may be somewhere where you will not be disturbed and where you can be alone with your thoughts. Which reminds me, you do not have to kneel or close your eyes when you pray. In fact prayers can be said anywhere at any time, no matter what you are doing. Maybe it's easier when you are alone and can concentrate, but nothing is to stop you saying a prayer when you are walking along the corridor at school or sitting on the bus on the way home.

Someone once said that basically prayer is talking to God. But that's not all there is to it. It is also about listening to God. You may say don't be crazy – how can you listen to God? Only people who are mad claim that God talks to them. Was St Paul crazy or Moses or Abraham? No of course they weren't. God does speak and we should listen. And how do we listen? Simple! Discover what love is all about because God is love and he puts his love in our hearts. So when we do something selfish or wrong it somehow does not feel right. It makes you feel uncomfortable and you don't feel good about it at all.

That is God speaking, showing you that love and friendship is greater and stronger than greed and selfishness. Let me put it another way. When we see something beautiful it makes us feel good and it inspires us. God is beautiful. In fact he is more beautiful than any precious stone or diamond ring. He is more beautiful than any snow-capped mountain or lush green valley. So he speaks to us not only through the beauty of all the created things around us but through the friendship of others and the care that he shows us through Jesus his Son. Jesus shows us what God is like. He came to show us what is good and true. So if you want God to speak to you look at all the beautiful things and the things that are so powerful like trust, love, truth, honesty and faith. And most of all look at Jesus because, as I said, he showed us by his words and actions what God is like and what he wants us to do with our lives in this his world.

I don't want to give you a long talk on prayer because prayer is simply talking and listening to God as you would a friend. But just to recap what I've said and add in a bit more, here are some guidelines about the different approaches to prayer.

SOME BRIEF GUIDELINES ON PRAYER

THE PLACE – Can be anywhere but best when you are alone.

THE TIME – Up to you. First thing in the morning or last thing at night. Basically any time you like, but try to make it regular.

WHO DO YOU PRAY TO? – God your heavenly Father who loves you and cares about you. He invites you into his presence.

WHAT DO YOU SAY? – Whatever you like. But best to include your thanks and gratitude. Mention your family and friends and mention your requests. Say sorry for what you have done wrong.

DO YOU HAVE TO KNEEL? – No. You can stand or sit. You can pray with your eyes open or closed. It doesn't matter.

HOW DO I LISTEN TO GOD? – By knowing the truth of God's love and asking forgiveness when you know you have done wrong.

DOES IT WORK? – The important thing about prayer is not getting God to do things for us but discovering what he wants us to do for him.

DOES GOD ALWAYS ANSWER PRAYER? — Yes, but God does not always give the answers we want. He always acts to do what is best for us. We cannot dictate to God what he should do. Remember even Jesus asked God if he could avoid the cross but God said no because through his death he was going to allow the most important event in human history to happen — Christ's death and Resurrection to new life.

2

What others have said about prayer

Seven days without prayer makes one weak.

Allen Bartlett

If you are swept off your feet, it's time to get on your knees.

Fred Beck

Prayer, in its simplest definition, is merely a wish turned God-ward.

Phillip Brooks

If you would have God hear you when you pray, you must hear Him when He speaks.

Thomas Brooks

Prayer is conversation with God.

Clement of Alexandria

Pray and then start answering your prayer.

Deane Edwards

Prayer is like the turning on of an electric switch. It does not create the current; it simply provides a channel through which the electric current may flow.

Max Handel

Prayer does not change God, but changes him who prays.   *Soren Kierkegaard*

Prayer at its highest is a two-way conversation – and for me the most important part is listening to God's replies.   *Frank Raubach*

The fewer the words the better the prayer
                                                Martin Luther

Prayer opens our eyes that we may see our selves and others as God sees us.   *Clara Palmer*

Prayer is dangerous business. Results do come.
                                                Christie Swain

Prayer is a rising up and drawing near to God in mind, and in heart, and in spirit.   *Alexander Whyte*

Prayer surrounds the world.   *Anon*

3

When you need help

DEAR LORD, take my hand and lead the way. Amen

Dear Lord, help me to be strong. Give me courage to face the future and to accomplish your plan for my life. Let me see the pitfalls and other dangers so I can avoid them. Keep my soul free from sin, my mind clear of evil thoughts and my body free from temptation. In your holy name. Amen.

Lord, are you really out there? Please listen to me. I'm confused, worried. I don't know what or who to believe. Do you hear me, understand me and care for me? Please help me Lord. Thank you. Amen.

Father, you and I have got a whole lifetime together.

Sometimes I reckon even that won't be long enough for you to straighten me out. But other times I don't know if I could handle all those years. Will I make it? Or will I lose faith like so many others? How do I know if I'm treading the right path or if I'm going off by myself again?

Help me to keep my eyes fixed on you Lord. Don't let me be distracted by anything else. For I know if I hold on to you I can live by faith and everything will turn out fine in the end.

✦

Father, when I am lost and lose sight of you, when I forget my prayers and I'm swept away with life and all its difficulties, when I cannot answer my friends' questions about my faith even though I know the answer, when I'm too busy, and like homework I cannot do, you get shoved to the bottom of the pile. Remind me that all I have to do is to STOP! For I know that you will find me and will meet me wherever I am.

✦

Dear Lord, my life is full of upsets. I often wonder if you are really listening. Please help me to be patient when I'm in a mess and listen to you. Please relieve me of any worries in my mind and help me to have faith in you and know you are always listening to our prayers.

✦

Dear Lord, I feel lonely and unloved by everyone. Help me to realise your love is everlasting and will never leave me. Help me also to feel your presence so that I can come through this hard time with your help. Amen.

Dear Lord, when I need you, be by my side to guide me. Hold me in your tender hands and hide me from the blinding light. Keep me ever safe and warm near you, love me, save me, help me. Draw me to your kingdom Lord and keep me ever faithful. Amen.

Father, so often we fail, not just in our own eyes, and those of others in this world, but most importantly in your eyes. Lord, help us to realise how much you really love us by giving us friends, families and the other wonders of your creation. Help us when we stray from your path and bring us back to your way of truth and love. Amen.

❖

4

When you want to
say thanks

DEAR LORD, Thank You. Amen

Dear Lord,
With tears in my eyes
I look out upon your world.
I see all the pain,
the hurt and sadness.
I see joy and love too,
and this joy and love keeps me going.
For love is from you Father,
given to us by your Son
who died for our sins.
Thank you for saving us. Amen.

Thank you Lord for being there
to help and comfort me.

I know I can always trust you.
If I'm in trouble, there you'll be.
In every stage of living Lord
you're always there to guide.
I hope one day I meet you
when you call me to your side. Amen.

I thank you for everyone who has taken part in bringing me to your presence, for my parents who brought me into the world and educated me in the ways of life, for friends who constantly uplift me when I am down or depressed, for leaders and fellow church people who provide much needed inspiration during times of trouble. However, help me to remember and in some way help, those who are less well off than me, those who lack a house, food or love from friends. In Jesus' name, Amen.

Lord God. Thank you for all your
blessings; for life and health,
for laughter and fun,
for all our powers of mind and body,
for our homes and the love of dear ones,
for everything that is beautiful, good and true.
Above all we thank you
for giving your Son to be our Saviour and Friend.
May we always find our true

happiness in obeying you,
for Jesus Christ's sake. Amen.

✤

Dear God, the Bible tells us to be joyful. Help us to
be glad you are in us and around us. You, Lord, are
the fountain of love which never ceases. Thank you.
Because of you we know that whenever we need a
friend or guidance you will always be by our side.
You are always ready to listen or to pick us up when
we are down. So Lord, we thank you. Amen.

✤

Thank you, Father, for all you've done for us. Thank
you that your Son went through all the agony and
pain of the cross to save us from our sins. Thank you
that you care for us, as your children. Thank you that
you love us, and know us. Help us, Lord, to get to
know you better. Thank you that you have sent us
your Holy Spirit to guide us. Please fill us with your
Spirit, Lord. Thank you for everything. Amen.

✤

Dear Lord God, I thank you that you are always with
me when I need you, always willing to listen when I
am talking and always speaking to me when I need
talking to. Amen.

✤

Lord, thank you for putting us in this world to serve and love you. Amen.

✣

Dear Lord, thank you for giving us this day,
our family and friends.
Help us to make the right decisions
for others and for ourselves.
Help us to be kind and good
and always have faith in you.
Give suffering people courage and strength,
to help them start anew.
Make us pure and forgive us our sins,
so that we may be like you! Amen.

✣

Lord in this life of ours,
We take little time to stop
And say 'thank you'.

✣

5

When you feel guilty

LORD, I KNOW I've done things wrong.
I don't want to admit to it;
neither to my friends nor family or you.
Lord it's hard to live with myself.
I want to ask for your forgiveness
but I feel I don't deserve it.
To be honest I don't deserve it.
But thanks to you I know it's still there for the taking
so I ask that I may be given a fresh start
and be directed again on the right path.

✦

Lord we confess that
when you call, we keep quiet.
When you beckon, we hesitate.
And when you repeat the call
we stubbornly stay silent.

We have sat content and unthinking
wrapped smug in ourselves.
We remain oblivious whilst others suffer
and are proud of our satisfaction.

Let us lay aside our petty arrogance
and take up the power of humility
So that we may learn
and come closer to you.

Lord, it's easy to laugh
So easy to hate.
It takes guts to be gentle and kind.
May we not be content with our frailty.

Let us not be blinded by
the trinkets of vanity
or intrigues of government
May we clearly see the path ahead;
the trail which was laid down by the one perfect
    sacrifice
along which we can follow your guidance
of justice and truth.

We confess our weakness
in not observing your example.
When questioned let us have the strength
to pass on your message.
Help us to answer your call. Amen.

When we have sinned against you, Lord, or any one we know, we feel guilty and ashamed at the wrongs we have done. We know that you will always forgive us, so please help us not to abuse your love. Guide us away from sin and the consuming self-hatred and guilt which ensue. Amen.

✤

Dear Lord, please cleanse me from my sins and forgive me for my wrong-doings. I am truly sorry. Amen.

✤

Dear Lord, when we have done wrong, the burden of guilt is like a heavy bag of grain which rests on our shoulders. You take this heavy load away, dear Father, when we ask for your forgiveness. Please help us not to do things which will cause a terrible pang of guilt. Help us to follow your path of love and truth. Amen.

✤

Please Lord, please help us not to sin or lie or cheat. Amen.

✤

21

6

When you feel lonely

LORD, friend to everyone, you know when I feel lonely and discouraged. Please help me to realise that I do not need to seek your presence, but that I am living in it daily and can never be alone. For your name's sake.

Dear Lord, thanks for always being there when we need you. Help those who don't know that you care for them and that you are always there. For those people who stand in the corner of the playground, who sit on their own in class, who go home to an empty house, who have no one to talk to and are LONELY, Lord help them. Help us to be friendly, not unkind, to talk to them, not ignore them. Amen.

Dear God, when I feel lonely or depressed, help me

to remember that you are with me wherever I am. You always know what I'm thinking and doing, so help me to feel your presence all of the time. Help me realise that you love ME as an individual despite everything, and that you will never stop loving me. Amen.

♣

O Father God, as you know
I haven't many friends.
Whenever I want some company
I only get dead-ends.
And so I come to you, dear friend
You never let me go.
I should have come to you first
But I just felt so alone.
So Father God, I ask you
to come and be my friend
and stay with me, O Father God,
beyond a long life's end.

♣

Lord, I'm lonely and I don't know who to turn to. I ask you to be with me, and with all people who are alone. To be alone is terrifying and everyone needs love. Comfort us, Lord God, for Jesus' sake. Amen.

♣

Dear God, when we feel alone, when there is no one

to talk to, when our lives seem empty and we need a shoulder to cry on, help us to remember you are always there, help us to turn to you as our friend and father. Amen.

Dear Father, when I am feeling lonely, please help me to find friendship. When I feel neglected and out of place, please help me to remember you are there. When I feel a misfit, or visit an unfamiliar place, please remind me O Lord that I will never be alone, you will always be my friend. Please help me to draw in and welcome those who are lonely and on their own. But most of all help me to tell others they won't be lonely if they love you. Amen.

If you are feeling really alone but there are people around you, you probably need some support and understanding. It's best to tell someone you know who will really sympathize and understand and try to help you. Possibly a best friend or maybe someone you don't know all that well. Then there is God, even if you are not aware he is there, you must have some idea, or you wouldn't be reading this. He can offer you support and comfort. Just by being relaxed and quiet by yourself you can gain inner peace, and that in itself will help.

I look up from my hurried task
and see no one there.
I stop and wonder where everyone is gone.
For me it is only a short while,
for countless others the feeling never stops.
It attacks day and night
cutting and bruising the fabric of the mind and
    body.
People are not made to be alone
and we have not the right to
subject anyone to that.
Pray God I will be given the strength
to befriend the lonely and give them comfort.
    Amen.

♣

7

When you feel depressed

THANK YOU LORD that you're always there when I feel sad or let down, because I know that you will never let me down. When life seems unfair I can always depend on you for your guidance and support to help me through difficult situations. Amen.

Dear Heavenly Father, why do so many people seem against me? Every way I turn it seems as though there is another figure to insult and hurt me. So often I fight back with fierce words which seem to come from the centre of my depression. Oh Lord, please help me to control myself in these situations and find the love from the centre of my heart to give them. Lord I always know that no matter how people turn against me, I will always have you as a friend. Amen.

Dear Lord, there are times in our lives when we feel lonely and depressed. Help to guide us through these dark times in our lives. When we are depressed remind us of that special love you have for all of us. You love us so much that you died for us.

Help us to remember this and to know that you will always be with us whatever happens in our lives. Amen.

✤

Lord, difficult situations appear every day that question our faith. To be unhappy is the worst situation I have ever faced. We love you with all our heart, how do we show our love when we are depressed? I am your sheep and I'm lost. Find me Lord. Amen.

✤

Dear Lord, when I feel depressed and think that nobody cares about me, help me to realise that there are many people around me who can help and who love me just like you do. Help me to turn to them and to you, when times are rough. You taught people to love each other. Help me to remember this when I feel depressed and out on my own. Through your name I ask it. Amen.

✤

Lord, I am sad.
I am crying.
Like dew on a web: help me find beauty in my tears;
beauty in my life.
Let me cry for ever.

✢

Dear Lord, help me to overcome depression. After all, when I think of the insignificance of my depression compared with the starving, abused and lonely I feel privileged. Please lift my thoughts and spirit up so I can do your work. Amen.

✢

8

When you want
to say sorry

LORD, help me to know when I am wrong and give me the strength and courage to say that I am sorry – three words that so often we find hard to say but can make such a difference to both our lives and to those we love. Help me to realise that our life on earth is far too short to argue with those we love and care for and that we should all have the compassion for others that you have for us. Forgive me Lord for all my wrongdoings and help me to be a better person. Amen.

Dear God, I'm sorry for all the times I do the things that I know you wouldn't want me to do. When I think or say something to hurt someone; when I fail you and fall short of your expectations. Help us to be more like your son, Jesus, every day. Amen.

Oh Lord, it is so difficult to say sorry to anyone and even more so to say sorry to you. It is impossible to find the words to express exactly what we feel but I pray that you will read our hearts rather than our words and hence discover our true sentiments so that you may know how sorry we are, Lord, for everything sinful in our lives. Amen.

Dear Lord, there are many things that we need to say sorry for. Maybe we have been selfish or hurtful, or misunderstood friends and family. Sometimes we say things on the spur of the moment which we regret later. Help us to be more controlled about what we say. Sorry is such a difficult word to say, so help us to say it openly and meaningfully. Amen.

Bad luck Lord, it's me again! Guess what I've done this time. — You know. Oh well then I had better just say I'm 'sorry'. Amen.

Dear Heavenly Father,
You know all of us.
You love all of us.
And care for each of us.
I do not know you well
and sometimes I forget you are here.

I am sorry for when I've forgotten you.
Help me to remember you are here all
the time, not just Sundays. Amen.

✤

God, I made a real mess again, didn't I. I never
intended to hurt anyone. I just didn't think. I ended
up hurting the people I love the most, including you.
But I think it was me who hurt the most in the end.
Sorry. Amen.

✤

Dear Lord, I know you don't want a great big long
explanation as to why I committed a sin *yet again* —
you know all that but what I really want to say is
. . . . Please forgive me. Amen.

✤

9

When you want to celebrate

GOD,

Let's celebrate!

Let's celebrate your love for us all, no matter who we are.

Let's celebrate our life on earth.

Let's celebrate our love for you.

Let's celebrate your giving to us your one and only son.

Let's celebrate love – our love for you and your love for us.

Without this love, what can we celebrate?

Lord, in your name. Amen.

Dear Lord, at this present time I feel so close to you. I can feel you in my life. At these times I want to celebrate, for your love is so strong. When I try to think of all the wonders you have performed my whole existence seems so trivial and when I think of all my sin I am so ashamed. But, Lord, you still love me and I am grateful for that. I am so glad that I have opened my heart for you. Without you, there would be no point for me to go on living. I want to tell everyone of your love so they can feel the warmth and security that I can feel at this time. Thank you Lord, and help me to remember that you are always there with me. Amen.

Dear Lord, we thank you for the power and love you give us. May we recognise how much you help us in everything we do and may we be content with all that we have and not always ask for more, as you give us all that we need. Amen.

Dear Lord, we celebrate all the things you have given to us. The sun, stars, trees and flowers. Also for all the people you have placed here on earth. Teach us to love them all and not just those we consider our friends. Please help us through our hard times and keep us safe in your love and security forever. Amen.

10

When your life is
really difficult

DEAR LORD, I am finding life hard and frustrating; nothing seems to work out right. I pray that your love and strength will sustain me through this time and that your spirit will guide me so that I become aware of your will and fulfil it to the best of my ability. Amen.

Dear Lord, we cannot possiby understand you fully, or comprehend the ways in which you work. When we are depressed, help us always to remember that you want what is best for us. Sometimes, the things we worry over turn out to be your way of bringing us closer to you. However sad or worried we are, and however far we drift away from you, your constant love is always there to aid us and bring us back into your presence. Amen.

Dear Lord, please help us to know that whatever problems we may have, we can always rely on you to help us. May we confide everything to you with open hearts and trust you to show us your unfailing love in our times of need. Amen.

❦

Father, my life is turning out a mess. Sometimes I wish I could just fall asleep and never wake up. But that would be a waste because, Lord, you have given us one life. Lord, help me to steer my life into a happy one. Amen.

❦

Lord, times are difficult. I need you Lord. I need to know that you are near, that you are watching over me and most of all, Lord, that you love me. Please guide me in everything that I say and do. Thank you. Amen.

❦

Lord, thank you that you are always with me, especially when I am going through difficulty. I thank you, Lord, that you experienced the difficulties of life when you came to live on earth, and experienced suffering when separated from your Father, I pray, Lord, therefore that you will guide me and lead me always, especially now. Amen.

Remove us, oh Lord, from the cynicism and hypocrisy of our secular preoccupations; and give us true faith which consists of sincerity in our love for all that is good, and for all that you have done for us. Just as your Son rose from the grave, give us the courage to rise from all the pride and pretence which so loosely clothes our sometimes empty souls. Help us to expose your true light, through our faith. Amen.

✢

O Lord, You have searched me and you know me.
You know when I sit and when I rise;
You perceive my thoughts from afar.
You discern my going out and my lying down;
You are familiar with all my ways.
Before a word is on my tongue
You know it completely, O Lord.
You hem me in – behind and before;
You have laid your hand upon me.
Such knowledge is too wonderful for me,
Too lofty for me to attain.
Where can I go from your Spirit?
Where can I flee from your presence?
If I go up to the heavens, you are there;
If I make my bed in the depths, you are there.
If I rise on the wings of the dawn,
If I settle on the far side of the sea,
Even there your hand will guide me,

Your right hand will hold me fast.
How precious to me are your thoughts, O God!
How vast is the sum of them!
Were I to count them, they would
outnumber the grains of sand.
When I awake
I am still with you.
Search me, O God, and know my heart;
Test me and know my anxious thoughts.
See if there is any offensive way in me,
And lead me in the way everlasting. Amen

(Sorry, Nick, I couldn't think of anything to write,
so I nicked this from Psalm 139! Sorry! This is what
I always read, when I feel low.)

♣

11

When you are doing exams

I PRAY that in the coming exams you will keep me calm and bring back to my mind all that I have learnt.

Dear Lord, help me when I feel panicky about my exams. Help me to realise that it only matters if the mark is good for me, not for anybody else. Do not let our parents get us down, saying we must get at least 99% in every subject in exchange for a new bike. Wish me luck. Amen.

Dear Lord, when I take exams let me go the extra mile with revision. I know that if I fail you will be there to say I haven't. When I'm feeling down about exams, help cheer me up. Thank you Lord. Amen.

Dear God, I have just had my exams, which I didn't enjoy, but you got me through them. You gave me the strength I needed and now I want to celebrate because I actually passed. I feel as if it were all worth it after all. Thank you for your strength. Amen.

Lord, my heart is pulsating and
My tummy is quivering and
my mind is whirring.
— Oh please! refresh me with your peace.
I pray, dear God, that as my exams approach,
I may feel calm,
Let your peace shine through me,
that others may glimpse the serenity within me,
and want to discover its source.
Please remove that ominous, depressive cloud
which seems to hover over exams, and replace it
    with sunshine.
Let me look foward to my exams,
seeing them as a time when I can share my
    knowledge of things with a, probably, weary
    examiner.
Please help me not to worry, Lord,
for worrying solves no problems
If my marks are good,
please help me not to rest on my laurels.
If my marks are bad,
please help me not to despair.

You love me, Lord, and I love you.
That is more important than any exam result.
Thank you for hearing me. Amen.

✤

Dear God, help us through this difficult time of exams. Help us to do as well as we can so that we can obtain the qualifications we need to do what you have in mind for us. We know that even if we do not do as well as we expected you still love us and still have a purpose for us. Perhaps you are teaching us patience by getting us to retake them or perhaps you have something entirely different in mind. If we do as well or better than we expected then we must remember that without you we would have got nowhere, whether we acknowledge it or not because without your gifts of life, intelligence, a conscience, and, of course, a soul, we are nothing. We pray that you may relieve the exam stress that affects so many people so that we can do our best. Thank you O God. Amen.

✤

Dear God, please help me through my exams. Stop me from cheating which wouldn't be right. I am hopeless at the moment, but would be more assured if I can send this prayer. Amen.

✤

Father, I thank you that you are always with me, especially when I am in difficulty. Guide and help me through these exams so that I may do justice to all I have learned, Lord. I dedicate them to you and pray that I do them for your glory and not my own. I pray for everyone doing exams and that you may guide and help all of them. Help us to keep their importance in perspective Lord and to use them to draw closer to you. Thank you. Amen.

Dear God, please help me in my exams. Help me to understand the questions. Amen.

12

When you are worried about others

LORD, some people really suffer because of something physically wrong with them and others suffer just as badly because of some mental disability. Please Lord, we know that with you we can help these people to fight their disability or illness. Strengthen us so that when we know someone who has something wrong with them we may have the faith to help them in whatever way you show us. Amen.

Lord, we think of young people all round the world especially those who don't know you, who don't have the opportunities to grow in your love. Help us, Lord, to share with others the knowledge of your presence in our lives. There is still so much about you we have yet to discover, give us the courage, Lord, to know you more and to show our faith in our everyday lives. Amen.

Father, I thank you for my friends. Without them I wouldn't be as strong, but Lord please teach me how to love without intruding, how to be gentle but sincere, to cope when all seems to fall apart. When someone I love is hurting I feel pain, also when someone is upset I long to help them. Lord, give me strength to be there when someone needs me. Help me to help them through their troubles. Speak through me so that I can be sure that what I say is of use. Help me to care rather than to worry for I know it's the caring and understanding that I need to give. Thank you for listening to my feelings. Father, I know I can help the ones I need to, with your strength and love. Amen.

✦

Father, there are times when I act by instinct and not by thought. But there are other times when I act on purpose to hurt. I am sorry for those times, help me to think and help rather than hurt those who are my friends.

As tears course down people's faces
Their pain is like a fire inside.
The fire will always be there,
It can only be cooled by the
love of dear friends.
The pain will always cause anger and grief.
The only cure is love and patience. Amen.

Heavenly Father, I am praying for people who are ill or sick. For people who do not have any money to buy food for their families. Those who do not have any family to turn to and who live on their own and have no one who cares about them.

I also pray for those who are depressed or unhappy at this moment.

For the children who have no mums or dads because they have died.

Please help them through this. Amen.

♣

Loving Father, we pray for people living on their own, who cannot get out and about. Please help them not to lose faith but get to know you more. Please help people not to be lonely, especially old people, or people who have been bereaved. Make them see that they can always find a friend in you, whatever the time, wherever the place. We ask this, in your name. Amen.

♣

Lord, help us when we are worried about others. Help us to comfort them. Help us to pray for them. And Lord help those who have any kind of illness. Amen.

♣

13

When someone
lets you down

DEAR LORD, why isn't everyone in the world like you? Amen.

Lord, only you know how much I am hurting inside and how unwilling I am to forgive. Help me to remember the sacrifice that you made for me by dying on the cross and to see that in comparison my sacrifice is small. Lord, help me to forgive those who have hurt me. Amen.

Dear Lord, as I speak to you now I feel hurt and neglected. Please help me, Lord, to understand why I was let down and please help me to forgive them as you forgave me. And please fill me and them with your everlasting love. I ask this in your name. Amen.

Dear God, when we are let down don't allow us to become bitter. Instead of turning away from someone, help us to see their reasons for doing what they did. You're the only one we can completely depend on. But don't let us dismiss others because of the human faults we all possess. Amen.

Dear God, please help. My friends have let me down badly. They have suddenly turned against me because of where I live. They call me names and tell me I don't belong. Please help me to overcome the hurt I feel. Thanks. Amen.

Dear Lord, when someone lets us down it seems so hard to be able to forgive them. Please help us to be able to forgive and forget and to say sorry when we let others down. Amen.

Dear Father, please help me forgive those who let down, use, or disappoint me: for you have often forgiven me for far worse things. Help me also to want to forgive them and to do it willingly without malice. Remind me in times of anger to remember that revenge does not do any good and help me to forgive and forget as our Lord Jesus Christ always did. Amen.

Dear Lord, when someone lets me down don't let me get annoyed; let me listen to their reason and be sympathetic. If they have an awful excuse don't let me question it for Lord if they lie they are only deceiving themselves. Let them see this. Thank you dear Lord. Amen.

✤

Dear God, when we are let down by a friend or relative, help us to be strong and help us to understand why we have been let down. If we are upset, help us not to forget that you are with us in whatever situation arises, and that you are there to assist us. Help us to remember that there may be more than just ourselves involved. Perhaps the culprit feels guilty, or maybe he/she has let down more than one person. Help us not to be too self-centred. Amen.

✤

Lord,
I've been let down
again. By one of my friends
again. He forgot to turn up
again. He was too busy
again. Didn't have time.
Lord I'm getting fed up
with excuses. I can't see what is so difficult about coming round to help me. If I ask you to help me you are there – so why is it so difficult for us to help

each other? Lord, I pray that I may be tolerant of my friends' shortcomings. Help me not to forget that I have just as many faults as anyone else. Teach us to be humble Lord, and always to remember we are all equal in your love. Amen.

❖

14

When you have doubts

DEAR GOD, we all find things hard to believe, and our minds are filled with doubts. Is there really a God? Did everything in the Bible really happen? Why do we believe in something we cannot see? God, you know that we do have faith, but the world's temptations often steer us away. Guide us away from those temptations. Fill us with your Holy Spirit to help us to answer our doubts and strengthen our faith and love for you and each other. Amen.

✝

Dear Lord, it is so easy to doubt you,
there are so many questions we want to ask.
Help us trust in you so that in time we will find
out the answers.
In times of worry and trouble,
when we need your love the most,
help us to feel your presence

so you can guide us in the right direction,
towards a brighter, happier and loving future.
Amen.

❧

Dear Lord, life is full of ups and downs and often I
am filled with doubts. Help me to trust in you and
to have a steady faith, to be child-like – not always
questioning but obeying. Guide me through
depressions and teach us to stand up against the
forces of evil and corruption, for I know that
nothing can separate me from your infinite love. In
Jesus' name. Amen.

❧

> God doesn't want you to have anything.
> He's not waiting for you to attain some goal.
> He's not comparing you with anyone else.
> You need to love him, to believe in him,
> to do what he wants.
> You need to see him as God.
> You may falter, fail and fall.
> Everyone else seems to be going along fine.
> Why me Lord? Why am I the only failure?
> Yet when He looks at you, he sees . . .
> No, not tangled mess, but gold.
> For your desire to know him better
> Is more precious than any achievement.

Ask for that desire to increase
for that is your God's delight.

Dear God, just about everyone has doubts but often
living away from home, especially for the first time,
can be an incredibly testing period. You find yourself
surrounded by strangers many of whom are not
Christian, and, because you so desperately want to fit
in, you may find your values begin to slip.

As Jesus suffered in the wilderness help us through
these times. Let us remember that there are always
going to be others in the same situation who need
our help. And let us remember that our Christian
roots are only a phone call or a letter away. But most
importantly you will never desert us. Amen.

Dear God, in times of doubt and hesitation please act
as our guide. When we are in darkness, then shine
like a lamp to light the right path. Help and advise us
when the answer to a problem seems unclear, for we
would all be lost without you and existence would
be in chaos if doubt were to gain the upper hand.
Amen.

Dear God, I know that I have my doubts about you,
that I am unsure when it comes to making a decision

at a fork in the pathway of life. Often I am tempted to take the easy route, almost always the route away from you. Help me to grow in your faith that I may make the right decisions and put your will before mine, to do your work in the world, for your glory. In Jesus' name. Amen.

✤

15

When you don't get on with parents

LORD, help me to restrain my anger and frustration when I have been arguing with my parents. I know they mean well, but they don't express their feeling of love and caring in the way I'd like. Help me to understand that they mean well and help me to go back and say I'm sorry. In Jesus' name. Amen.

Dear Lord, there are times in my life when I feel everyone is against me, especially my parents. They seem to be so nasty and are always criticizing my actions. I know they are only trying to show me the right way to live but it's very frustrating being ordered about. Help me to honour and respect my parents, to give back a little of the love they show for me, to obey and not to question. For it is in giving that we receive and in pardoning that we are pardoned.

I pray these things in Jesus' name. Amen.

✤

Dear God, please help me to make amends with my parents. They make it difficult for me and I cannot help disagreeing with them. Please help me to see things from their point of view. Thank you. Amen.

✤

Dear God, please let my parents realise how much I love them and do so want to get on with them. I know I have been bad but they just don't understand my feelings. Amen.

✤

Dear Lord, Our Father, please have pity on me and my family,
for we fight with wrong in our minds and not right.
We fight without concern for other people and later we regret it.
Give us wisdom, faith and trust in our family. Amen.

✤

Lord, help us to get on with our parents at all times. When in time of stress let us be able to comfort each other. Help us to understand what they are feeling when we annoy them. Let us be loving and

cherishing, able to respect and be grateful to them at all times. Help us to obey them and not to answer back when told to do something we don't like.
In your name. Amen.

✤

O Father, why is it when at our age if you hit your brother or have an argument, your mother shouts at you and you don't get a word in edgeways? When this happens I don't want to take the law into my own hands.
Please help me. Amen.

✤

16

When you are afraid
of the future

DEAR LORD, when we are worried and afraid of the future, not knowing where we are going to go, or what we are going to do, please guide us along the right path and reassure us that you will look after us, whatever happens in the dangerous road of life.
Help us to keep faith in you, and know that we always have a place in your heart. Amen.

Dear God, at this moment in time the future seems frightening but I know you have a plan for each and every one of us. Lord, help us not to be afraid of the future and give us faith to trust in you Father. I love you. Amen.

Dear God, when we are afraid of the future strengthen our hearts and minds, and give us courage

to face up to whatever lies ahead. Let us remember
that you will always be there with us shining your
light before us. Amen.

Lord, you have shown us a way
for us to live from day to day.
But 'money talks';
'on yer bike!' (and all the rest)
is what they say
and think is best.
Even though, Lord, you might
not like our ways of greed and plunder
or even wonder
why we always have to fight.
So show us, Lord, your way of life
in this absurd and crazy world
with love in our hearts
and peace among us. Amen.

Lord, please help me when I am afraid of the future
to be guided by your word
to walk ahead with confidence into the darkness.
Give me courage to carry on
and strength to take step after step
until I emerge on the other side
with a greater love of you. Amen.

Lord, help us to put our faith in you, and let us trust you to take care of our future. Whatever the situation let us look to the future hopefully, knowing that you will always be there to help us in times of trouble. Amen.

✛

17

When you have got an important decision to make

EENY MEANY MINEY MO,
Help me find the way to go. Amen.

Father, you know that I am afraid, and I don't know which way to turn. Please Lord, come down and comfort me, and help me make the right decisions. Please Lord, help all those who are going through the same experience as I am. Give them strength through your Holy Spirit. Lord, I ask this in your name. Amen.

Please Lord, this decision could be a turning point in my life. Shine your light to show me the right path to take. I know that you will show me the way. I know that you will always be with me, loving me, and I trust you to show me the right path. Amen.

Complete Prayers for Teenagers

Lord, when we have a difficult or important decision to make, please help us to make the best and wisest choice. If the decision is going to hurt, let us forget about it, or if it is for the good of others, let us stick to our decision, through to the end. Amen.

✛

Lord God, we are making decisions every day. Important decisions can often tell you where your life is going to lead. Help us to make the right decisions Lord, so that we may follow you in the ways of your Son. Amen.

✛

O Lord, I pray that you will be with me to help and guide me whenever I have to make an important decision in my life. I know that I can trust you to be by my side to give me the strength and help that I will so often need.

I also ask Lord that you will help me to be grateful and cheerful for all the wonderful things in life that you have given to us, but we so often take for granted. Help me to remember that you are always there when I need help and that you know which road is the right road for me to take. Lord hear my prayer and always be by my side. Amen.

✛

18

When you are grateful for your friends

LORD, thank you for my friends. Thank you that they are always there when I am in trouble and need help, or when I need a shoulder to cry on. Help me to be loyal to my friends and to give them as much love and support as they give me, not only in times of need, but also when life seems to present no problems. For your name's sake. Amen.

Lord I thank you for my friends.
When I am confused
they give me wisdom.
When I feel sad
they help me smile.
When I feel worthless
they share their love.
Lord above all this,
I thank you that you are my
friend forever. Amen.

Dear Father, I thank you for all the friends you have blessed me with. I am grateful for their witness of you, their support, and love in times of suffering and despair, and for their presence to share in times of joy. Amen.

✤

Friends are to be trusted,
friends try to be kind.
I thank you Lord for friends.

Friends are to be treated nicely
and not to be hurt or insulted.
I thank you Lord for friends.

Friends are more important
than personal belongings.
Friends are worth more than money.
I thank you Lord for friends. Amen.

✤

Dear Lord, when we are spiteful and nasty to our friends,
help us to tell them how sorry we are,
for where would we be
without friends? We would be lonely and unhappy.
Jesus had lots of friends, even the outcasts. As you will always be our friend, let us love you as we love ourselves.
And let us be happy. Amen.

Thank you God for friends. Friends who stand by you in your time of trouble, who guide you through difficult decisions. Friends who tell you things that you should not do, and tell you when they don't like the things you are doing.

Lord, help us to accept our friends as they are, with all their faults. Help us Lord to forgive our friends who have wronged us or hated us. Help us to share the gifts and things we have with others, as well as our problems, as friends can prove very helpful and understanding. O Lord, help us not to be jealous of others and the friendships that they have. Make us grateful for what we have; help us appreciate this and be content with it. Amen.

✤

Dear Lord, we thank you for the friends we have and all the love and joy we share. May we learn how to be the best friends possible, and never expect too much from others.

Thank you for being our greatest friend, Lord. Amen.

✤

19

When others suffer
for their faith

LORD, thank you that we live in a country where we have the right to speak our mind and worship you our King without any restrictions. Teach us to remember all prisoners who suffer for their beliefs. And especially let us remember people who suffer in South Africa because of their colour or race. Let us remember all who suffer in Communist countries for their beliefs. We thank you Lord that we can worship you without being persecuted for it.

Lord, don't let us forget Christians in other countries. Amen.

✤

'If you encounter evil and refuse to oppose it, you surrender your humanity.

If you encounter evil and oppose it, you enter into humanity.

If you encounter evil and oppose it with weapons of

God, you enter into divinity'.
Father, fill your people with the strength of your love, so that through times of suffering their faith may prove strong enough to act as a shield against the burning arrows of persecution.

Dear Jesus, sometimes I take for granted the easy life I lead as a Christian. Although at times I may find it difficult to cope with situations that occur, and I question my faith, I know that in other countries people are suffering brutally for living their lives according to their faith. Help me not to be afraid to show everyone that I believe in you, and help others who are not afraid to do this, but suffer for it. Amen.

Dear God, you have given me the chance to meet with other Christians of my own age. When I see your light and feel your warmth in these people, I am strengthened. But this does not occur all over the world and not always throughout this country. Help me to remember those who are persecuted either physically or emotionally for their faith. Strengthen those living under repressive governments, and those who are ridiculed either by friends or in the home. Never let us forget these people. It may happen that we will find ourselves in a similar situation one day. And if we should, never let me deny that you died for us. Amen.

Dear Lord, I know that the persecution that I am experiencing is hardly anything compared with what Jesus and some other people in the world have had to put up with, but still it is hard to confess my faith in front of non-believers. Please Lord give me the strength that I need to be a true witness for you. Amen.

✤

20

When animals suffer

THANK YOU for all your creatures. Animals are a wonderful part of your creation, and so please let us appreciate them, and love them as you do. Let us not abuse them or make them suffer for our benefit. Cruelty is a major event in people's lives. So please help us to prevent cruelty in our world because everyone has a right to live, including the animals that you have made. Amen.

Dear Father God, you gave each animal a name and gave it life like us. They are so like us yet not so, as you gave them no voice that we can understand and no knowledge that they can understand *us*. For this reason we should communicate with them through love and affection, and respect their lives here on earth as our own.

We need help, as we too often take for granted our

power over animals. Help us not to abuse this power but to care for the creatures you have given us – after all they were created by you. Amen.

✤

Dear Lord, please help the animals who suffer whether through bodily harm or through lack of care. Please help the people who kill animals for fun or for their fur to understand what they are doing. Thank you for all the charities who help to make animals' lives better. Amen.

✤

Dear Lord, this is a prayer for those who cannot speak to save themselves from being destroyed. This is for the animals of our world who suffer because of humans whose only aim, it seems, is to expand and in doing so destroy the beautiful environment and animals you created for us. So help us to realise what we are doing or what we have already done. Help those who go purposefully out of their way to kill animals. Help us also to find other means of doing experiments without the use of innocent animals.

Lord, help us to think more clearly and carefully about what we are doing to the creatures of this world and our environment for the sake of those who cannot speak for themselves. Amen.

21

When the environment is neglected and destroyed

FATHER, we belong to you,
you made us,
you gave us life,
you love us.
Father, this is your world
you made it,
you gave it life,
you care for it;
yet we are destroying it.
We pull down the homes of the animals you created,
we burn the trees that you sent the sun and rain to
nourish.
Forgive us Father,
show us how to make your world
flourish,
not die. Amen.

Look at your beautiful earth Lord, look at what we are doing to it. An earth that you created especially for your children, a paradise for our time on earth and yet we neglect and destroy it.

Lord help us to be thankful for what you have given us – to respect our surroundings and to do our utmost to preserve it. For in guarding what you give us Lord, we are praising you for it. Amen.

✤

Dear Lord, you created the environment for us to live in, the green trees and grass, the blue sky and the sparkling sea. You created it to provide homes and happiness, yet we destroy the trees, we build factories where fields should be, we pollute the air with fumes, and we dump our rubbish in the sea. Why Lord do we do this? Please help us to treat the environment with care and respect, so that we can all live in a cleaner, healthier place. Amen.

✤

Lord, when we neglect and destroy our environment we also destroy your creation. Help us to look after our world, care for all that is in it and to show you that we are proud to be your children and live in your world.
Through Jesus Christ our Lord. Amen.

✤

Dear Lord, please help us to tidy up our town
(village, city) and countryside,
and make it look more respectable.
Help us to plant flowers
and tidy up existing flower beds.
Help us not to drop litter
but to put it in bins where it belongs.
Help us to do all these things and more. Amen.

God, you gave us this world to look after.
You put your trust in our hands.
You let us take care of your creation.
You gave us animals of all colours, breeds, shapes
and sizes.
You gave us beauty in our own surroundings.
You gave us colour and the blooming flowers of
spring.
You gave us a heaven on earth,
but we have to ask for your forgiveness.
We have taken your trust for granted.
No longer do all the animals roam the earth free
and in the right surroundings.
We kill them for the colour of their fur, or for their
elaborate feathers.
We kill them for money and selfish greed and
destroy their surroundings.
We erect miles of concrete and destroy trees and
plants which stand in our way.

We build for ourselves and destroy other living
   things for our comfort.
Not only do we destroy the wildlife, but we destroy
   each other.
We let each other starve, live in poverty, we kill
   each other, we steal from each other – but what
   for? – greed and money.
God we have turned the planet earth into a bomb
   of another kind;
not a bomb owned by the government, but a bomb
   every person owns.
The time for that bomb going off is getting near.
God, guide us and forgive us – please. Amen.

✤

22
Advent

DEAR LORD, thank you for this time of Advent. As we enjoy the preparation for Christmas, the fun and laughter, may we remember the true meaning of this time in the Church's year. Help us to let the light of your Son into our lives today. For your name's sake. Amen.

Dear God, as we begin our preparations for Christmas, help us to remember what Christmas is really about. As we light our advent candles, or our christingles, help us think about Jesus as the light of the world.
Without him there would be no Christmas.
Make us strong as we go through Advent and help us to think about Jesus, the Son of God, at his birth. Amen.

Dear God, during Advent we think about the coming of Christ. We pray to you to help us to keep our thoughts on the real meaning of Advent and to look forward to when Christ comes at Christmas. Amen.

Dear Lord, in this time of Advent, help us to prepare ourselves for Christmas. Help us to be guided by you as Christmas arrives, and in the hustle and bustle of preparation let us sit down quietly for a while to think about the real meaning of Christmas and Advent. Advent is not only a preparation for Christmas, but a time to remember Christ's promise that we would return 'like a thief in the night'. We must be ready for him always as we do not know the time or the place when he will come again. Amen.

Come, oh come Lord,
Lighten our darkness
With your word.
Strengthen our weakness,
Inspire us to praise and love you
And bring us your understanding. Amen.

✦

Dear Lord, during this Advent time help us to prepare ourselves not only to receive you as a small child in Bethlehem, but also as a great judge who will one day return to judge us all. Lord, we cannot say for sure when you will return. We can only ask that you help us to prepare ourselves to meet you. For your name's sake. Amen.

Dear Lord, help us to prepare for the coming of Jesus. Lighten our hearts with his Spirit and let him come to us and grow with us like a new born baby. This is a happy time at which I am proud to be part of the church. Thank you for guiding me towards this happiness and leading me to Jesus at this time. Amen.

23

Christmas

IT'S CHRISTMASTIME.
The holly is abundant.
The presents are under the tree.
The turkey is in the oven.
The grandparents are in the spare room.
But what of the meaning of Christmas?
'Yes, you know Jesus'. 'Jesus who?'
Father, let us not get carried away by the trappings of
Christmas.
Let us remember the birth of your son, our Saviour.
The traditions of Christmas may be fun, but let us
not forget the meaning of Christmas.
In Jesus' name. Amen.

❖

Dear God, at this special Christmastime help us to
remember the truth behind the festival. We praise
and thank you for sending your son to us. As he

came in humility, may we remember those less fortunate and more humble than ourselves. Amen.

❖

Lord, bless everyone this Christmas who won't be having a good time. People who are ill or in hospital. People who are on their own with no family. Fill their hearts with happiness so they can share in the true meaning of Christmas. In the name of Jesus. Amen.

❖

Dear Father, as we prepare for a time of giving and goodwill, help us to remember that Christmas is not just lights, presents and a stocking. There is a deep and wonderful meaning: a celebration of the birth of a little child whose words would far exceed the power of any leader and whose teaching is passed from generation to generation. This surely is the true meaning of Christmas. Amen.

❖

Peace, perfect peace?
A pretty strange idea Lord. No matter how many people strive for peace their work is soon undone by the weakness of man. But what sort of peace? World peace? Peace with yourself? Peace with God? Lord, help us to work for peace. To reconcile nations, races, cultures, creeds and neighbours that all men

may see eye to eye and call each other 'brother'; that we may all find peace in our hearts and peace with you.
Peace on earth. Amen.

✦

24

New Year

HEAVENLY FATHER, through your Son a light has shone upon the world, a new hope has touched the hearts of many. As we start a new year be with us in all that we think, say and do. Help us to act upon what we believe and not lose sight of your wondrous love for us.
Through Jesus Christ our Lord. Amen.

Dear Father, I pray that as a New Year approaches you will strengthen my faith and commitment to you. I pray that you will help me to be more compassionate, patient and tolerant towards others. I pray that you will guide me in all that I do and help me especially as I try to spread your word, in the most tactful way, to others who may be unsure about their belief in you. I ask this in Jesus' name. Amen.

Dear God, let the New Year be a new starting point. A point to forgive and forget the things people have done against us and a time to look back and learn from our past mistakes. Let us also look forward to the future and help us to aim for the right things, and give us a purpose to live for.

✤

Father, we thank you for helping us in times of difficulty over the past year and for being with us. Help us to go forth into the New Year knowing that our faith will deepen and our love for you will grow stronger. Be with us when we are having fun and when we are unhappy. Now and forever. Amen.

✤

We thank you for this opportunity to begin again – for a fresh start, so that we can forget what has been bad and remember the good; so we may lead a new life, with you to help us on our way. We ask you to guide us, taking each day as it comes. Amen.

✤

Father, as I throw off the old year and with it all its sins, tears and confrontations, help me to go forward; forgiven, cleansed, refreshed, to make a new start full of confidence to do what I know to be right, to fight for justice, to take up life's challenge and to win. Amen.

Dear God, thank you for all the good things that have happened, like the help countries have given to the needy and the efforts to make the world more at peace. Help and strengthen these efforts. Please comfort all the people who where involved in the tragedies and violence of the past year and guide them through the New Year. Amen.

Dear Lord, as we come into a New Year may we pray that it is a successful one for all of us whether we are at college, university, school or in work. We pray for all teenagers worldwide and that you will guide us with your hand through any decisions we have to make concerning our future. Amen.

25

Lent

DEAR GOD and Father, as we start this spiritual pilgrimage of Lent, help us to resist the temptations of the devil and to persevere through the wilderness of this world. Help us to appreciate how lucky we are as we embark on seven weeks of self-denial and to use your faithful Son Jesus as an example and guide.

Help us to think about why we give up things and make sacrifices and let this period be a time for reflection so that we may be open to the true meaning of your death upon the cross, for us, and the resurrection to new life on Easter Sunday. Amen.

Dear God, help us in this time leading up to Easter to remember why we celebrate Easter, not for the commercial reason, but for you. You gave away your life for us and for this we are grateful. Amen.

Father, at this time, where by tradition we 'give up' something, let us begin something new that will aid others. Amen.

Dear Father God, when we go out into the wilderness as Jesus did, on our own in this huge world, keep us free from temptations and sins. It is easy for our minds to be distracted so we fall into the wrong path. At Lent especially give us strength to persevere, and to give something up, not because we have to but because we love you. Amen.

Dear Lord, make this time of self-denial, when we give up something that is going to help us deepen our life with God and grow closer to him, a meaningful experience. Amen.

Dear Lord, Easter is coming soon when we remember the death and resurrection of Christ. In the days leading up to Easter, we think about the agony Jesus went through knowing he would die. So as we give up various things for Lent we look forward to the day when Jesus rose again. We ask you now and for always to look after us like you did your son. Amen.

Dear God, at this time of self–denial, let us remember the words of your son Jesus Christ. 'Do not sleep, get up and pray that you will not fall into temptation'. Give us the strength to perform the tasks you set for us and give us the courage to stand up for your love. For the sake of Jesus. Amen.

✤

26

Easter

DEAR LORD, thank you for Easter Sunday. The sorrow and the sadness of Lent and Good Friday is gone and is replaced by the happiness and rejoicing of Easter.

Now to some the true meaning of Easter is in the background, replaced by chocolate eggs, and the coming of spring.

But I try to remember Jesus and what happened on Easter Sunday, and love you for it. Amen.

Dear Lord and Father, we praise you for sending your son to us in human form to die for our sins. We pray that from Christ Jesus' death on the cross we may learn to open our hearts to you and place you first in our lives so that we may have eternal life. Thank you Lord. Amen.

Dear God, thank you for sending your son to us, to teach us about love and the Holy Spirit. He died for us on the cross; for this we are grateful. Help us to remember this brave act of love. Amen.

Lord, at this time we thank you for your son Jesus Christ, who died for our sins and we thank you that he has risen again. Amen.

Father, thank you for all you have done and all you have given us. Thank you that at this time your son died to save us and conquered death. We can now be reconciled to you and live with you in your glory because of the ultimate sacrifice your Son made for us. We thank you Father and Lord. Amen.

Dear Lord, when you gave us Jesus you must have know what we'd do.
When we tortured him and wanted him dead, you should have been enraged. And yet I know you love us because you let us do all this and then gave us yet another chance when he rose again. Amen.

27

Pentecost

DEAR LORD, in the same way that you touched your disciples with the Holy Spirit, kindle your fire within our hearts so that we may be able to accept you as you show yourself to us in our everyday lives – whether it be through friendship, worship or just the peacefulness of prayer. Amen.

Dear Lord, long ago, you started the church when you sent down your Holy Spirit upon the twelve disciples. Help us to realise that we too can experience the same joy today that they experienced by receiving your most precious gift. We know that you will always be there and all we have to do is call on you. Thank you for this. Amen.

Dear Lord, at this time of Pentecost at the coming of the Holy Spirit let us celebrate.

You died, you conquered death and you rose again for our salvation.

You filled our hearts with the Holy Spirit, giving confidence to call you Father.

You gave us the chance to teach your word and spread the Christian faith; help us to use this power and not let it slip away. We can then make disciples of all nations, baptizing them in your love.

Like Thomas, help us to combat our doubts and have faith that you will always be with us to the very end. Amen.

✢

Lord, thank you for sending your Holy Spirit to strengthen, help and guide me. It's so wonderful knowing that a part of you is with me always helping me to come closer to you. Amen.

✢

Dear Lord, thank you for giving us the strength and power to deal with all situations in life through the power of your Holy Spirit. We pray that just as those early Christians received your Holy Spirit so may we also receive HIM. Thank you Lord. Amen.

✢

28

For the Church

SOMETIMES, Dear God, Church is unbearable but at other times it's really alive. Keep the source of this mighty river of Christianity full of love and welcome. Amen.

✤

Dear God, thank you for the Church, for the whole lot of friends we make through it, and for being our friend. Amen.

✤

Dear Father, we pray for strength and unity in the Church throughout the world, especially in places where other conflicts hinder its growth and blot out or destroy the message that we are trying to spread. Amen.

✤

Father, when people see the Church they see bishops in ornate robes and architectural wonders.

Open their eyes Lord, and let them see your Church, the living Church, people, millions of people, all over the world, ordinary people in ordinary places loving one another. Amen.

♣

Dear Father, thank you that as well as giving us our natural families you made us part of your family, the Church, that we might meet in fellowship and gain encouragement by being with other Christians.

Please help the members of our church to come closer together in unity and understanding. Amen.

♣

29

For the youth group

DEAR LORD, thank you for youth groups. It's great to know that we can meet with other Christians and share our faith together. We praise you Lord. Amen.

✤

Dear God, you have brought many young people together of all nationalities to share your love. Each time we meet our love grows stronger. Be with us in our youth groups and help us to learn and understand your ways. Let our faith ripen in the unity of fellow Christians and let our love for one another grow each day. Help us all to live by your teachings and guide us along the right path. Amen.

✤

Dear Lord, I pray now for our youth group. It is so encouraging to see so many friends enjoying themselves together. Help us to spread your love.

Give us strength Lord to teach others your word.

I thank you for the leaders who give up so much of their time for us and I thank you that we are able to meet together freely.

I hope that our group will grow in your Holy Spirit and may your love be shown on all of our faces.

I pray for all the other Christian youth groups in the world.

Help them all to find your love. Shine your light upon us.

Lord, in your name. Amen.

❖

Dear God, we thank you for our youth group. Although we may not be very large, we all take active parts in helping the Church. Help us to know and understand more about you so that we can spread your word to others, particularly people our own age. Help us to make others welcome so that we may become bigger and stronger. Thank you God. Amen.

❖

Thank you Lord for the various organisations to which we belong, especially the Brownies, Guides, Cubs, Scouts and Boys Brigade. Thank you for the people who lead us and put a lot of time and hard

work into these activities. May your Holy Spirit guide them in all their preparations.
In Jesus' name. Amen.

✤

Father, through you our youth group was formed, through your love you have bound us together. We share many wonderful and fulfilling friendships and you give us time to be together and energy to enjoy that time. Thank you for the leaders who help us and encourage us.

Lord give us the strength to include anyone who is new or lonely, let us be gentle and warm so that they will feel comfortable and a part of our group as we know how important the feeling of being included is. Thank you for the chance to praise you together. Amen.

✤

Dear Lord, we know that you are always with us. When we come together you rejoice. Help our youth group always to renew and reaffirm our commitment to you whenever or wherever we meet. Help us to value the time and friendships we make and guide us so that we may all follow the way to you Lord. Amen.

✤

30

Some famous prayers

LORD, make us instruments of your peace.

Where there is hatred, let us sow love;
Where there is injury, pardon;
Where there is discord, union;
Where there is doubt, faith;
Where there is despair, hope;
Where there is darkness, light;
Where there is sadness, joy;

O Divine Master, grant that we may not so much
seek to be consoled as to console;
to be understood as to understand;
to be loved, as to love;
through the love of thy Son who died for us, Jesus
Christ
our Lord. Amen.

St Francis

Some famous prayers

O God, give us

Serenity to accept what cannot be changed;
Courage to change what should be changed;
And wisdom to distinguish the one from the other;
Through Jesus Christ our Lord. Amen.

Reinhold Niebuhr

> Day by day, dear Lord, of thee
> Three things we pray:
> To see thee more clearly;
> To love thee more dearly;
> To follow thee more nearly;
> Day by day. Amen.

St Richard of Chichester

Christ has no body now
  on earth but yours.
No hands but yours,
No feet but yours;
Yours are the eyes
  through which is to look out
Christ's compassion to the World;
Yours are the feet
  with which he is
to go about doing good;

Yours are the hands
  with which he is
to bless us now.

St Teresa of Avila

✣

Christ be with me, Christ within me,
Christ behind me, Christ before me,
Christ beside me, Christ to win me,
Christ to comfort and restore me.
Christ beneath me, Christ above me,
Christ in quiet, Christ in danger,
Christ in heart of all that love me,
Christ in mouth of friend and stranger. Amen.

St Patrick

✣

Teach us, good Lord
To serve thee as thou deservest;
To give and not to count the cost;
To fight and not to heed the wounds;
To toil and not to seek for rest;
To labour and not to ask for any reward,
Save that of knowing that we do thy will. Amen.

St Ignatius Loyola

✣

O gracious and Holy Father,
Give us wisdom to see thee,

intelligence to understand thee,
diligence to seek thee,
patience to wait for thee,
eyes to behold thee,
a heart to meditate upon thee,
and a life to proclaim thee,
through the power of the Spirit of
Jesus Christ our Lord. Amen.

St Benedict

Give us O God:

Thoughts which turn into prayer,
Prayer which turns into love,
Love which turns into deeds. Amen.

Eternal God and Father,
you create us by your power
and redeem us by your love:
guide and strengthen us by your Spirit,
that we may give ourselves in love and service
to one another and to you;
through Jesus Christ our Lord. Amen.

Our Father in heaven,
hallowed be your name,
your kingdom come,
your will be done,
on earth as in heaven.
Give us today our daily bread.
Forgive us our sins
as we forgive those who sin against us.
Lead us not into temptation
but deliver us from evil.
For the kingdom, the power, and the glory
     are yours
now and for ever. Amen.

❖

MORE PRAYERS
FOR TEENAGERS

What is prayer all about?

MEN AND WOMEN down the centuries have discovered that prayer is a very crucial part of life. Without prayer, life can be very hard and dry. But when we pray something very special happens which we may not always be aware of. We are allowing God to come particularly close and we share with him the things which are of real concern to us. In a way we are allowing God to look into our hearts and our innermost feelings. We are sharing ouselves with him. When we allow God to come close to us and when we look at him then we see our lives in the right perspective and this breathes spiritual life back into us. It brings us alive again and puts us in touch with God in a fresh way. Prayer can make such a difference and no one can expect to live the Christian life without making prayer a priority. So what is prayer all about?

Prayer begins with God. It is he who is our Father in Heaven and is the one who knows us by name and loves us. He has made us his children and therefore if we want our relationship with him to grow we need to talk to him. You cannot expect any friendship to develop if you do not talk to the person concerned. You have probably experienced with some of your friends that if you do not keep up with them by talking, phoning and seeing each other, then your relationship will drift apart. It can be very difficult, as you may know, when you move house. At first you are very keen to keep in touch with friends from where you previously lived, but as time goes on inevitably the strength of your friendship can weaken. So if we want to keep our faith and friendship with our Father strong we need to talk frequently with him. We need to keep in touch. Prayer begins with God because it is he who first offered his friendship to us. He wants to come alongside us and share his love with us day by day. You may have a special friend whose company you really value and enjoy. When something happens or you have some particular news, they are the first person you want to tell. In many ways this is how God feels about us. He is delighted when we come to him and he is anxious to give his love to us through our friends, through the gifts we may have and the things we enjoy. If you look at the beauty of creation you can see that God is trying to communicate to us that he has given us a special world to live in – a world of colour and light and amazing complexity and variety. When God created the colour green he was not content to have all the fields and trees of one shade. Instead, because of his infinite imagination, he gave us more variety of that one colour than we would have been capable of thinking of. It is this God who is concerned for both the great and small, the finite and the infinite, who wants us to renew our friendship with him day by day by sharing our thoughts and prayers with him. Prayer begins with us recognizing all that God has done for us in creation and salvation. The sad thing is that we often spoil the things he gives to us. But he does not reject us because of that, but rather calls us to come closer to him and live our lives the way that is best and the way that was originally intended

Prayer is simply talking to God. It is focusing our thoughts and minds on him. When you talk to someone you turn and face them and look at them. You give them your attention. You look at them and they look at you. Prayer is turning towards God.

Prayer brings you closer to God because there are just the two of you talking together. It can be a very personal and intimate experience.

Have you ever had an audience with the Queen at Buckingham Palace? You will probably say 'no' and it is not very likely that you ever will. However, you never know, one day in the future you may be called to the Palace for something special you have done. Who can tell what may happen in the years to come? If you do go for an audience you would not expect just to drift in and pull up a chair. You would come in reverently, acknowledging whose presence you were in. In the same way, when Jesus taught his disciples to pray he said that we should first acknowledge who God is. That is why he said we should begin by saying, 'Our Father who art in heaven, hallowed be your name . . .'. In other words, we acknowledge that it is God who is our Father and Creator, and because of that his name is to be praised and revered. He is our Lord and Ruler who is concerned about us and welcomes us into his presence, so we should give him the respect that he deserves. God is indeed our friend who is always with us but we should never treat him disrespectfully. We should always be mindful of who he is.

WHAT SHOULD WE PRAY ABOUT?

Well, what should we talk to God about? Of course about our concerns, but we should begin by giving thanks for all that he has done for us. There are plenty of things we can thank him for – our life, food, health, parents, friends and family. There will always be something positive, something good we can give thanks for, even when life seems very difficult and painful. In fact if you give just a little thought you can probably think of a multitude of things, both great and small, that it is worth saying thank you for.

There is nothing worse than someone who is ungrateful. If you have ever experienced a friend who takes you for granted and never appreciates what you do for them you will know how difficult it is. It may not be that you want any sort of praise for what you do for them but just a "thank you" would be really appreciated. How do you think God feels at times when we do not show any sort of appreciation or gratitude? I'm sure he feels painful about it. This is why it is important that we give thanks to God. So make time in your prayers to say "Thank You". Show your appreciation to God in the way you most enjoy. You don't have to be quiet and serious if you do not want to be. I'm sure that the worship in heaven is not always quiet. Have you ever been to a pop concert? I'm sure that you will say "yes" or that at least you hope to go one day. The great thing about concerts is that they are usually very noisy affairs with a lot of energy, lights and enthusiasm. You become caught up in the whole experience. You can feel the music and it is almost as if you can see the sound hit the roof and reverberate about the building. I believe that the worship in heaven is often like a concert, full of energy and vibrancy.

God wants us to worship him sometimes quietly and reverently but sometimes with a loud voice as well. We may at times feel we want to shout his praises from

the rooftops, thanking him for all he has done for us.
If you feel that way at times do not think that it is
inappropriate, because look at what the Psalms say:

> Clap your hands, all peoples!
> Shout to God with loud songs of joy
> For the Lord, the Most High is terrible,
> a great king over all the earth.

If in your prayers you want to shout your thanks to
God, then do it. Mind you, it might be diplomatic
to make sure that you will not disturb someone else
in doing so?
What should you do next?

PRAY FOR YOUR FAMILY
AND FRIENDS

Pray for your Mum. Pray that God may bless and
strengthen her in all the work that she has to do. Ask
that your relationship with her may grow and deepen,
that you may have a better understanding between you.
Then try and make life easier for her by offering some

practical help. Make your bed. Tidy your room. Ease the hassle that makes things difficult at times. As one Christian said, "Pray, then start answering your prayers".

Pray for your Dad. Things may have been difficult at work with various pressures and important decisions that have to be made. Or maybe your Dad doesn't have a job; this brings worries all of its own and causes great anxiety. Pray for him and take the trouble to find out what he may be concerned about. If it is appropriate, ask him what he would like you to pray for, that can be a great help. Pray also that your relationship may improve and grow stronger. Dads as well as Mums are very special, so they deserve your understanding and your prayers.

You may not get on well with your parents at times and things may be quite difficult at home. But prayer can help. It can help you see your parents as God sees them and in a better light. It can help you understand what they feel. It is actually not easy being a parent. It can be very hard work, and sometimes you do not make it any easier. So show your love and care and ask God to bless your family.

Then there are your friends and their ups and downs. It's great to have friends. Life would be terrible without them, though at times you may think you would be better off! But just imagine if there was no one to share things with and to talk to. Life would be very cold and lonely. So pray for them and the things that concern them. Prayer can be so important because it strengthens our relationship with our friends. It shows that we are thinking of them and wish that only good should come their way. Prayer can make a relationship special and it's great to be able to pray for our friends because of the strength and help it can give to them. You may also find it helpful to get together with a friend once a week or possibly once a month and pray together. Jesus promised that where two or three are gathered together in his name then he would be in their midst. So when two of you agree to pray together, Jesus is with you and praying together can be very helpful and effective. Why not try it!

LORD, I'M SORRY

Prayer is also concerned with saying sorry. Sometimes you may not tell the truth or deliberately distort things so as to get out of a difficult situation. You may, like all of us, be unkind and selfish to others. When this is the case we cannot come to God in prayer as if nothing has happened, rather we need to ask God to forgive us. If we say we are Christians and yet we do not live a Christian life then we are betraying ourselves and the God we believe in. It is good to stop for a few moments in your prayers and recall the things you know that you have done wrong. Possibly you were bad-tempered with someone or said something cruel behind someone's back. Maybe your thoughts were filled with sexual fantasies which you know were wrong. All these things we need to confess to God and ask him to forgive us. If we allow our sins and wrongdoing to go without confessing them to God then they will spoil our relationship with him. However, if we tell God what we have done wrong then the wonderful thing is that he will forgive us. We need not then walk around with a continual feeling of guilt, because once God has forgiven us he does not hold our sins against us, in fact he forgets about them completely. No matter what we have done or how bad it is God will forgive us if we ask him, and because he forgives us he wants us to forgive others.

PRAYING FOR THE WORLD

It is important in your prayers to look beyond your own world and think of those in the wider world. Traditionally in church we pray for the Queen and members of her government as well as the world leaders, that there may be peace and co-operation between peoples and nations. In your own prayers remember the people you have seen on television or read about in the newspaper who particularly need prayer because of something that may have happened to them. Often when I'm watching the news I pray for the people I see who have suffered some tragedy, or I pray for the family of someone who has been killed. I remember on one occasion feeling very strongly that I should pray for someone who was shown on the news and who had been a victim of a terrorist attack. Fortunately the man survived, but afterwards I discovered that the man was a Christian so it made me realize how important prayer can be.

MAKING SPACE FOR PRAYER

Prayer is also about being quiet at times. Things may be noisy at home, so where do you go to be quiet? If you are fortunate to have your own bedroom then it may not be a problem to get a little bit of privacy. But let me make a few other suggestions which you might find helpful if it is difficult to find space at home to pray.

- Going for a walk can provide the opportunity to be alone to think, reflect and pray. Is there a park or pleasant walk near you which would be suitable?
- Take off on your bicycle to somewhere which you know will not be disturbed.
- One very easy way of finding space is to drop into church. You will usually find that one of the side chapels is an excellent spot to do some thinking and prayer. If your church is often kept locked, ask your Vicar if you can borrow the key. He would probably be delighted to know that you wanted to use the church.

If you give it a little bit of thought you can probably think of quite a number of times and places where you can go to be quiet and alone with God. Jesus would often try to get away from the vast crowds that followed him so that he could have the opportunity to pray. It is amazing in many ways, because it is so tempting to fill our lives with being busy all the time, particularly if people need our help. Despite the fact that Jesus was desperately needed and sought by so many people he realized that it was of crucial importance to go and spend time with his father. If Jesus needed those times with God when he could renew his spiritual strength, then you and I need to do the same.

One problem about making space for God is not just finding the time and place – that can be easy if we get our priorities right – but how to keep our minds on our prayers. Sometimes when I start to pray I suddenly find my mind invaded by a dozen other thoughts of things I need to do or something I've forgotten. It is a common problem, which I'm sure you have experienced as well. If my thoughts are wandering all over the place I find it helpful to hold a cross in my hands. If you do not have a cross of your own, make one. If it is just a very simple cross of two pieces of wood you have put together then that would be suitable. Some friends of mine find it helpful to light a candle and to watch the flames as they pray. It gives them a sense of peace and reminds them of the serenity of God. Mind you, if you do use a candle it might be diplomatic to have a word with your mother beforehand, in case she is anxious about any accidents.

It is good to have somewhere to pray that is quiet and where we can be alone with our thoughts, but prayers can be said anywhere at any time. There is nothing to stop you praying as you walk along the corridor at school or on the way home on the bus. Prayers can be said anywhere. They do not have to be said with your eyes closed or when you are kneeling. I often pray when I am driving along in the car. Closing your eyes then is strongly not recommended!

LISTENING TO GOD

Prayer is basically talking to God but it is also about listening to God as well. You may say, "Don't be crazy, how can you listen to God? Only people who are mad claim that God speaks to them." Was Moses mad or Abraham or St Paul? There may be times in our Christian lives when, like some of the characters of the Bible, we hear the voice of God. You may have already experienced that. God does speak to his children and we need to listen. How then do you discern between what are your own thoughts and what is the Spirit of God leading and directing you? Firstly, nothing that contradicts the teachings of the Bible will be from God. So if you feel that God is speaking to you, check it out with what the Bible says. Secondly, do those who are more spiritually mature and who are in a leadership position in your church agree with what you think God is saying? God does not speak to people just for their own benefit, so never go and do something on your own. If you feel God is calling you to help with the Sunday School, start a prayer group, or be involved in some act of service then always talk to someone else about it.

You may still ask the question "How do we listen to God?" God is love. We grow in our Christian lives as we learn to love God and love others. If we do something that denies that love, such as being selfish or immoral, then the voice of God through our conscience will tell us that we are wrong. We will feel uncomfortable and lacking in God's peace. That is God speaking, showing you that love and friendship is greater and stronger than greed and selfishness. Let me put it another way. When you see something beautiful it makes you feel good and inspires you. God is beautiful. In fact he is more beautiful than any precious stone or diamond ring. He is more beautiful than any snow-capped mountain or lush green valley. So he speaks to us and inspires us not only through the beauty of all the created things but through the friendship of others and through the care he shows us through Jesus his son. Jesus shows us what God is like. He came to show us what is good and true. So if you want God to speak to you, look at all the beautiful things in life and the powerful things such as trust, love, truth, honesty and faith. And most of all look at Jesus because he shows us by his words and actions what he is calling us to do today in his world.

Listening to God in our prayers is very important. It also takes time and experience to know how to discern the voice of God. Talk to your Vicar or youthgroup leader about it and don't be afraid to ask any awkward or difficult questions.

HELP! PRAYER IS DIFFICULT

I hope I have not given you the impression that prayer is always wonderful and an easy thing to do. You probably know that it is not. Prayer is difficult. Often you are tired, you have been under a lot of pressure and you do not feel like praying. It is easy to skip praying one day and before you realize it a week has gone by and you have not done any serious talking to God. There can also be times when our routine is upset, such as exams, family holidays, illness, moving house, to mention just a few reasons. Virtually every Christian I know, including myself, has gone through times when they have not prayed. So if you feel a failure at times because you have forgotten your prayers, then join the company. However, if we realize that we have not given prayer the priority that it should have in our lives, the thing is not to give up due to guilt, but rather to start again. You can do that by setting yourself achievable goals. Aim to pray every day for five minutes. Don't feel you have to measure up to other people's spiritual achievements. If they pray for twenty minutes every day – fine. But that does not mean you are a failure if you only pray for five. There is nothing worse than setting out with unrealistic expectations of what you are going to do and then not being able to stick to them. So be reasonable. Try to make the effort to pray for a period of time you know you can manage. Even if it only for two minutes that is better than not praying at all.

There will be occasions when prayer comes very easily and you think that you have got it worked out. But there will also come times when it will be very difficult and you will feel that you are doing it out of duty. This is normal Christian experience. The important thing is not to give up but to be persistent. Often the most worthwhile things in life have to be worked at because they do not come without effort. So stick with it, the benefits and value are enormous!

SOME BRIEF GUIDELINES ON PRAYER

THE PLACE – Can be anywhere, but best when you are alone.

THE TIME – Up to you. First thing in the morning or last thing at night. Basically any time you like, but try to make it regular.

WHO DO YOU PRAY TO? – God your Heavenly Father

who loves you and cares about you. He invites you into his presence.

WHAT DO YOU SAY? – Whatever you like. However, it is good to express your thanks and to mention your family and friends. Say sorry for the things you know you have done wrong, and finally express whatever is concerning or worrying you.

DO YOU HAVE TO KNEEL? – No. You can stand or sit or walk or run or be lying in bed. It does not matter what posture you are in when you pray. You can pray with your eyes open or closed, there is no strict rule.

HOW DO I LISTEN TO GOD? – By knowing the truth of God's love and seeking to obey his will in all things, and by allowing ouselves to be still and receptive to the Holy Spirit.

DOES IT WORK? – The important thing about prayer is not getting God to do things for us but discovering what he wants you to do for him.

DOES GOD ALWAYS ANSWER PRAYER? – Yes, but God does not always give the answers that we want or expect. He always acts to do what in the long term is the best for his children. We cannot dictate to God what he should do. Remember, even Jesus asked his Father if he could avoid the cross, but he said "no". Often we look for the easy answer to a problem. But God's ways are not our ways. All we can do at times is just trust him.

WHAT OTHERS HAVE SAID ABOUT PRAYER

Seven days without prayer makes one weak.
Allen Bartlett

If you are swept off your feet, it's time to get on your knees. *Fred Beck*

Prayer, in its simplest definition, is merely a wish turned God-ward. *Phillip Brooks*

If you would have God hear you when you pray, you hear him when he speaks. *Thomas Brooks*

Prayer is conversation with God.
Clement of Alexandra

Pray and then start answering your prayer
Deane Edwards

Prayer does not change God, but changes him who prays. *Soren Kierkegaard*

The fewer the words the better the prayer.
Martin Luther

Prayer opens our eyes that we may see ourselves and others as God sees us. *Clara Palmer*

Prayer is dangerous business, results do come.
Christie Swain

Prayer at its highest is a two-way conversation – and for me the most important part is listening to God's replies.
Frank Raubach

SOME PRAYERS WORTH LEARNING

It is always worthwhile knowing a number of prayers which you can use when it is appropriate. This can be helpful when you are not sure of what to say and when you cannot find the right words to express what you feel. Here are three prayers which may be helpful, but I suggest that you find a number which you particularly like and learn them.

> Day by day, dear Lord, of thee
> Three things we pray:
> To see thee more clearly;
> To love thee more dearly;
> To follow thee more nearly;
> Day by day. Amen.
>
> *St Richard of Chichester*

O gracious and Holy Father,
Give us wisdom to see you,
intelligence to understand you,
diligence to seek you,
patience to wait for you,
eyes to behold you,
a heart to meditate upon you,
and a life to proclaim you,
through the power of the Spirit of
Jesus Christ our Lord. Amen

St Benedict

Eternal God and Father,
you create us by your power
and redeem us by your love:
guide and strengthen us by your Spirit,
that we may give ourselves in love and service
to one another and to you;
through Jesus Christ our Lord. Amen.

A.S.B.

Part One

PERSONAL

I

For when you want to give thanks ·

DEAR LORD, YOU gave so much for us and you expect so little, thank you for being there when I need you. You are my guide when times are hard and you are also there to celebrate the good times of life. Thank you. Amen.

Father, I just want to thank you for the fact that however upset, confused or feeling left out I may be, you are always there for me to turn to. Thank you for giving me strength to face up to my problems and talk to my friends. I also pray that they too will be able to find your comfort and peace. Amen.

O God, thank you for cricket, thank you for football, thank you for television, thank you for living.

Our Father, as we talk with you now, help us to give you thanks for this world and for our family and friends. We thank you for your generosity in giving us your Son who died for us. But Father, when we do not know how to thank you or what to say be with us and understand. Thank you. Amen.

Dear Lord, thank you that you are there in times of trouble to lead us, guide us and even pick us up when we have stumbled and fallen. These are all the characteristics of a good friend and you, Lord, are the best friend anyone could ever have. Thank you, Lord, for just being there when we need you. Amen.

Thank you, Father, for the gift of knowledge; knowledge brings with it reason and reason is a great tool. It creates an atmosphere of understanding which leads to caring, which is love. Knowledge also brings the responsibility of sharing it. Give me time, Lord, to share what knowledge I have gained, always remembering that people are more important than time. Lord, although I keep on learning more about you, I am thankful that there is a depth to you that I will never understand. There are deep truths that are beyond human ability to grasp. Thank you, Father, for knowledge. Amen.

Dear God, thank you for always being there. Amen.

Dear Lord, I just want to thank you for always being here with me when I'm at my lowest and when I'm at my happiest. Thank you for being the best friend anyone could ever hope to have and for loving me just the way I am. I do not deserve your love and I'm grateful for everything that you do for me and everyone else. Thank you, God. Amen.

Dear Lord, thank you for giving me the life that I have. Help me to be thankful and not take things for granted. When I argue with my mother and father, forgive me and help the family to get back together again. Amen.

Father, thank you for the opportunity of talking to you and getting to know your will and purposes through prayer. May we realize the importance of this communication with you and let us never be discouraged. Help us put time aside each day to speak with you. Thank you, Lord. Amen.

Lord, thank you for dying for us. By the perfect sacrifice of your body and blood, you give us the opportunity to be forgiven and to be reunited with

God our Father. Help us, like the Apostles, to trust and believe in you, though we cannot fully understand the mystery of this sacrament. Amen.

Dear Heavenly Father, thank you so much for friends, for the love and enjoyment they give us, helping us through the bad times and the good. Please help us to be sensitive to them and be caring and kind when they too have a problem. In your name. Amen.

When we think of all the things you have done for us, we feel very humble. For the way that you love us and for dying for our sins we want to thank you and worship you. When we think that you made us and the world we live in and everything around us we know that your power is never-ending. Thanks. Amen.

Help me to remember how lucky I am to have parents and enough food and water and a good home. Help me to remember that there are people in this world that do not have the lovely things I do. Amen.

Dear Lord, at the end of another day help me to thank you for all you have done. Help me to be caring towards others and treat them as I'd like them to treat me. Lord, please take my life and help me to live it the way you want me to, and to obey all your commandments. Lord, I ask this in your name. Amen.

2

For when you want to
say sorry

PLEASE HELP ME Jesus. I hurt someone today and I didn't mean to. Please forgive me. Amen.

Sorry for all the times I've wandered from your pathway. Sorry for the days when I've ignored you. Sorry for the times when I have not listened to your word. Sorry for the moments when I've chosen my own way. Sorry for the times I've forgotten about you, but you remain at my side. Amen.

Lord, so often I mess up and do what you don't want me to. It's a huge comfort to know that you forgive me and love me, even when I may not be able to forgive myself. Thank you, Lord. Amen.

Dear Lord, please forgive me for what I did to my best friend today, somehow I want to make it up to them, but I don't know what to say. Please be with me, Lord, when I try and put things right. Amen.

Lord, give us the courage to say sorry when we do things wrong and help us to bear the responsibility of all our actions towards others. Help us to be kind to our friends and not provoke anger in others. Amen.

Lord Jesus, the scorning past and the daunting future merge together at the present. I'm stuck. I've done the wrong thing I know. Help me to have the courage to offer my sincere apologies and others to have the tact to accept them. Amen.

Dear Lord, sometimes saying sorry is the most difficult thing to say. Help us to overcome our pride and selfishness and bring back into our lives those who are precious and dear to us by saying we are sorry. Amen.

Dear God, thanks for being a loving and forgiving God. We do so many bad things and yet if we say we're sorry we're forgiven, just like that. Help us to forgive each other just as easily and to understand someone else's point of view. Amen.

Streams of obscenities flow around my friends. They flow from us and over us. Their seed is within my heart and has grown. Forgive me for my sin for the pain and passion I have caused. I pray that my mouth may flow with the words of your voice. That my heart will beat in time with your own, and that my actions will be born out of love. For love I have found in you and I wish to share this joy with others. Amen.

Lord Jesus, I know I disappointed you today, and if I were you I would not have been forgiving. I am sorry Lord, and I know you'll forgive me and that makes me feel great. Thank you, Lord.

Dear Lord, you know how I'm feeling. You know when I'm busy and don't seem to have enough time for you. I'm sorry, Lord. Help me to become aware of and come closer to you. Give me the opportunities to help others to come to know you, and be with me as I grow as a member of your family. Give me courage to stand up for my faith – and thanks for just being there. Amen.

Lord, help me to admit when I am wrong and be able to recognize my faults. Help me to put this recognition to full use by saying sorry to those that I have offended. Help me to have an open heart and to find the right words. And help those to whom I apologise to accept my apology with a Christian spirit. I ask this through Jesus Christ, our Lord and Saviour. Amen.

3

For when you are grateful for your family and friends

LORD, THANK YOU for my friends. Life without them is unthinkable. They make me laugh and cry, they listen and they care. Your love flows through them. Thank you for the fellowship we can share together and the knowledge that you will always be with us. Amen.

Heavenly Father, I want to thank you for my friends. I thank you for their support and comfort in times of trouble and for their presence to share in times of joy. Lord, I pray that I would not become possessive of my friends and that I would be there with words of comfort when they suffer times of hardship and despair. Lord, I thank you for my friends and I ask that I would not take them for granted. In Jesus' name. Amen.

Father, I thank you for our friends.
They help us and are kind and caring.
When we are upset, they cheer us up.
Without them we would be lost.
Help us to be helpful, kind and caring to them..
Help us to cheer them when they are upset.
Help us to reassure them when they are worried.
And help us to be a faithful friend to them. Amen.

Dear God, thank you so much for my friends, that I have people to confide in and people who care for me. Make me a good friend so that I have the wisdom to help and support them in all that they do. Help me to understand and never to become jealous of my friends, and Lord, remind me that you will always be my friend even when others desert me. Amen.

Lord, thank you for the love and protection of families. Their care and never-ending concern, and just knowing that they are there for me is amazing. Thank you that friends also provide support and happiness. Lord, you provide so much goodness, thank you that you care so much about our life on earth. Amen.

Thank you, God, for giving me such wonderful friends and family. I am very grateful for what I have. I wish

everybody had such happiness in this world. I am very
lucky that I have such kind, understanding friends and
family. Thank you, Lord. Amen.

Dear Lord, thank you for the friends that everyone
needs. Help us to strengthen our relationship with
special friends, and help us to trust and respect and be
loyal to them. Give us strength when times of hardship,
depression and any other troubles strike, and help us
to stand by each other. Amen.

Dear Lord, look after my friends and the people I have
got to know so well. Help them always to put you
first and to realize what a difference you can make in
their lives. Help me to be a good friend to others and
always to have the time for them if they need it. Thank
you for all our friends and family. Amen.

Thank you for friends we can love and care for.
Nobody is able to love you fully, Lord, but give us
the opportunity to try. Amen.

Father, I thank you for my friends, without them I
wouldn't be as strong. But Lord, please teach me how
to love without intruding, how to be gentle and sincere

to cope when all seems to fall apart. When someone I love is hurting I feel the pain as well. When someone is upset, I long to help them. Lord, give me strength to be there when someone needs me. Help me to help them through their troubles. Speak through me so that what I say is of use. Help me to care rather than to worry, for I know it is caring and understanding that I need to give. Thank you for listening to me, Father. I know that I can help my friends when they need me with your strength and love. Amen.

4

For relationships with your girlfriend or boyfriend

LORD, HELP MY relationship not to interfere with my relationship with you. In the end I want yours to be the most important relationship in my life. Amen.

Dear Lord, make our friendship with a boyfriend or girlfriend to be loving and caring. Please blend our hearts together wherever we are, at school, home or church. Amen.

Dear Father, many of us have friendships with both sexes. We are lucky that we can share the good and bad times together. We know that our friends will care for us and help us through our troubles. Help us to see how important friends are and help us stick by them. When we do have a serious relationship do not let us forget those other friends who love us and need us. To the greatest friend of us all. Amen.

Loving Lord, help me please to tell the difference between real love and lies. It's impossible for me truly to love someone who is false because real love is not deceitful and brings only truth. Amen.

Lord! help . . . my friend has just left me . . . I cannot handle it, Lord, being so alone, just me. Yes, I know that you are always there so please send down your Holy Spirit to be close to me in my time of trouble. You know how much my ex. has upset me, so I pray to you now for help. Amen.

Dear God, we are grateful for all the things you have done for us, particularly in giving us friends and those who may be our girlfriends or boyfriends. Help us to be wise in all our friends and to care for others as we would want them to care for us. Amen.

Thank you for bringing us together. Please bless this relationship and help us both to develop the qualities we need. So that we can appreciate the good things such as understanding when sometimes things are difficult, consideration for each other, trust when we feel jealous, and love and care to strengthen our friendship. Amen.

Part Two

DIFFICULT TIMES

5

For those coping with divorce

LORD, DON'T LET people be worried about talking to you and asking you for help. When my parents divorced, my world caved in for months. I was scared of asking you for help in case I sounded selfish. But you never let me down. Even now I need to talk to you about my parents. It seemed you were the only one who cared about me. But you taught me to trust and love my parents again. Thank you, for ever. Amen.

Lord, we pray for those going through divorce, and having to cope with the hurt and rejection it brings. Give them courage and strength in their hour of need, and give them hope for the future. We pray that you will help them, that they will always have you and your everlasting love. Amen.

❖

Lord, when my parents split up, I felt lost, unloved, alone. I felt that for some reason it was my fault. I thank you that although some may fall in and out of love, your love is everlasting however bad I feel. Amen.

Lord, we pray for all those going through the pain of divorce, especially we pray for the children of the families as they see their parents argue because of the friction caused by the long legal process. Give them the strength to carry on. Give parents self-control so that the divorce can be settled peacefully, and give strength to other married couples to carry on through troublesome times. In Jesus' name we ask this. Amen.

I can't believe it, Lord. My parents are divorcing! Help me, please God, through this troubled time. Believe me, I need it. Amen.

Father, please help and support children whose parents are coming to terms with divorce. Help the children realize that it is not their fault, and that both their mother and father love them and need their support. Amen.

Lord, it's hard to cope when families break up. Often it's the children of the marriage who feel most let down. Please help all children, and indeed adults in these situations to know that you will never let them down and that you will be with them always. Amen.

Dear Lord, although you put together many families some of them split and it can leave hatred and anger. We just ask that you will help the parents and children involved in a divorce. Please be with them and help them in this time of distress and trauma. Please calm everyone and help them to get over it and lead their everyday life again. Amen.

6

For those doing exams

DEAR LORD, PLEASE be with me when I am in the exam room sitting at my desk writing away. Please help me, Lord. Amen.

Dear God, at this time I ask you to stand by me while I take my exams. When I get nervous, calm me down. When I get upset, help me to remain happy. And, Father, help me realize that you are always there for me to turn to. Amen.

Dear Lord, the pressure of exams can be daunting and stressful – it can seem like a never-ending tunnel of darkness. Help us to realize that you are the light of the world and that your love shines in us always. We can only do our best, so help us to realize that this is good enough for you. Amen.

Dear Lord, when we're preparing for exams and taking them we feel they will never end and that what we have done is never enough. Help us to realize that exams are not the most important thing in life and that you will lead us the way you want us to go, even if this means being disappointed with the results at the time. Thank you that you are always there when we need you. Amen.

I can't wait to finish the exams, Lord. When I get the results back please give me your peace, no matter what they're like. Don't let me forget that you'll never leave me and that your love for me has got nothing to do with how I do in the exams. Amen.

Dear Lord, I know you are there watching over me all the time, guiding me through good and bad times, giving me strength to do all that I do. I ask you, Lord, especially to help me throughout my exams when I need you most. Help me to persevere through to the end and give the best performance and to keep calm at all times. Thank you, Lord. Amen.

Father, thank you for the opportunity to learn and gain knowledge. In this trying period of exams, please help me to do my best, but not to crowd you and others close to me out of my life with work. Help me not to be disappointed with my results and not to reject those who have not done as well as I have. I ask this through your Son. Amen.

Dear Lord, please guide me through this time of exams. Help me to be calm throughout and to work to my best ability. Strengthen me as I do last-minute revision so that I can achieve the results I deserve. Lord, I know that you will be with me in these exams, guiding my mind in the right directions. Help me to know that you will always be with me. Amen.

7

For when you or your friends feel sad or down

LORD, YOU KNOW that as teenagers we are changing
from children to adults. Our emotions are unreliable
and change depending on our mood. When we are in
a mood of depression and cannot "snap out of it" help
us to feel that you are there with us. Touch us with
your Holy Spirit so that we feel happy again. Amen.

Dear Lord, this is a small prayer when my friends or
I feel sad. I know that when we are sad we need to
talk to someone about it and it is not always easy. I
would like to thank you that although I cannot always
talk about some things with my friends I know that
you will always be there for me. Amen.

Father, I thank you that you are always with us and
will never let us down. Sometimes life seems really

difficult, and there seem to be no easy answers to our problems. I thank you that you understand what we go through, and that you can support us and help us. Enable us to give all our problems over to you and trust in your answers. Through Jesus' name. Amen.

Lord, at the moment everything I do appears to be wrong. Whatever I turn my hand to it doesn't go according to plan. Why is life so difficult? Please Lord, help me through this difficult patch. Each day guide me along the pathway and give me grace. Help me to be brave and to remember that I'm much more fortunate than many others. In your name. Amen.

Dear God, help us to get on with our friends and help us to forgive them if they hurt our feelings. Amen.

Lord, when I am unhappy, pick me up. When I am losing faith, show me the path to your love. When I am upset, help me to get through it, and when I am happy, rejoice with me. Amen.

Jesus, I'm really depressed. Why did it have to happen to me? I may have made a mess of things, but I didn't really deserve it. Or did I Lord? Amen.

Dear Lord, there are times when we feel that everything is against us, when we feel that no one appreciates us or cares. These times make us feel alone, insecure and unhappy. But Lord, you are always there to help us and love us and you never turn your back even when we sin. Help us feel your presence, Lord, at times like this and to love and appreciate you. Thank you. Amen.

Dear Lord, help those who feel sad or down, for people who worry over things large and small. Let them know that you are always there whenever they need you. Amen.

Dear Lord, when we are feeling depressed help us to remember all the wonder of your creation, the delicate creatures you have created and the awesome landscape of the world. And above all, Lord remind us of the everlasting love you have shown us. In God's name. Amen.

I have a friend, Lord, whom I love so much, they are hurt, confused, mixed up, frightened and angry. How can I help them? What can I do? They need love and understanding. They need you. They are crying out for help. They cry out for love but there is no one there – except you. Help me to show your love to them and ease their pain. Amen.

8

For your enemies

LORD, I PRAY that in this world of hate, when someone hurts us in one way or another, you will give us the strength, and the sense of mind to turn the other cheek and forgive. Also when someone thinks of me as an enemy, I ask that you may help me love them back. Amen.

Dear Lord, help us not to think wrongly of others. Help us to see that they too have people they find hard to get on with. Help us to turn wrong to right and to join in with others. Amen.

Dear Lord, help me when friends tease me and wind me up, so that I don't lose my temper and say things that could hurt. Help me to show that same love that you give to me. Amen.

Dear Lord, we pray for all our enemies, the people we don't particularly like or get on with and who stress our nerves. We pray that we will try to be more friendly towards them and not exclude them in any way. In Jesus' name. Amen.

Dear God, please help me to become friends with my enemies and help me to be nice to them even if they are horrible to me. Amen.

Dear Lord, help us to see the beauty within all people and not judge a person from their appearance. Amen.

Lord, help us to think before we react. Help us to think about others and not just ourselves. Make us understand how others feel instead of abusing them to make us feel tall. Lord, in your mercy: Hear our prayer. Amen.

Holy Father, draw my enemies closer to you. Amen.

Dear Lord, please help me to get on with other people. Help me to see their point of view, especially when it is different from my own. Help me to consider others' advice, and help me to ask for it when I'm unsure. Let them know that they can trust me, and help me to learn to trust them. Amen.

Lord, it's hard to be with people, it's difficult to communicate. It's not easy to love, care and respect others. Sometimes we try too hard, sometimes we give up altogether. Lord, we know that you will always love us, so may we learn to love each other. Amen.

9

For when you are afraid of the future and have important decisions to make

DEAR GOD, THINKING about the future can be so daunting. On the one hand we're full of all the possessions we're going to acquire and the places we're going to see. And there is all the uncertainty about jobs, careers and domestic life. Guide us and help us choose the right path to go. Amen.

Dear God, the future is getting nearer and I'm getting more afraid. Exams are important. What if I fail? What will I do in life? In ten years' time where will I be? Not only are we afraid of our own future, but the future of the world. We are destroying your creation out of greed. Our environment is very important yet we are killing it. Help us, Lord, and guide us towards renewing your world. Amen.

Jesus, I know that you are there at all times, loving me and protecting me. Thank you that my destiny is planned and you are always in control of my life. Thank you that in times of trouble, hurt and need, you are standing there with your arms open wide, ready to hold me and comfort me. You are the only thing in my life which I can depend on to be there at all times, ready to pick up the pieces when my life seems in shatters. I love you so much. Please guide me along the path you want me to go. In your name. Amen.

Dear Lord, thank you for being with me in all that I do. Guide me so that I find the right road. Help me to be more understanding to other people's problems. Amen.

Heavenly Father, send me out into the world in the power of your Holy Spirit to work for you, to strive for peace and to complete the task you have set for me. I sometimes get worried about the future but I will try to trust you as much as I can. Reassure me when I doubt and correct me when I stray. I know that I'm here for a purpose, so please let me fulfil that. Amen.

Dear Lord, help us to be confident and have courage towards obstacles in the future. Please guide us in the right way and help to avoid bad temptations. We have to try not to fill ourselves with anxiety and to put on a brave face as we face the uncertainty of the future. We must try to remember that you are with us all the way. Amen.

Dear Father, as time draws on and our love for you extends, help us to deal with life in troubled times, so that our love for you wins through. May the future be bright and happy so that we can celebrate your love and care. Give us faith to trust in you, for we are your children. Amen.

When I'm scared of the future, comfort me and let me know that you are there all the way. Amen.

Lord, we have to make many choices and decisions in our lives, some more important than others. Guide us in the right way to make the best decisions. Amen.

Heavenly Father, I pray that you will guide me as I make this important decision. Let me put all trust in you and follow your lead in whichever direction it takes me. Strengthen me with your Spirit after the decision is made, so that I feel sure that I am following your will, especially if I'm not really sure that the right decision has been made. In Jesus' name. Amen.

10

For when relationships are difficult at home

DEAR GOD, WE know that sometimes we argue with our parents because they have said or done something we don't agree with. Help us to try and see their point of view and to see how difficult being a parent is. Amen.

Dear Father God, when I need guidance and I'm in trouble please help me through. I know when troubles and arguments occur in my family you are there to help. When I fall out with friends and feel lonely, you are there to help. When work seems endless and worthless, you are there to help. I thank you, Lord, for always being there to help. But please guide me to help those who have problems big and small. Amen.

Dear God, sometimes it is difficult for us to appreciate the love and care of our parents, especially when we are not allowed to do something. Help us try to understand that our parents are trying to guide us through the bad things in life and to help us deal with everyday problems. Father, help us to understand this when we are feeling down. Thank you, God. Amen.

Lord, I thank you for parents. I thank you that they *do* know what's best for us, however many times we think otherwise, and that they are always there to support and encourage us. Father, I pray that we'll reach the realization of how much our parents do love us, and how much they are prepared to do for our well-being. I pray, Lord, for the times when things aren't going well, that we would learn from the experience and grow to love and respect our parents more. Amen.

Please be with people who are finding life at home hard and distressing. Pour your love over them, so that they can love each other. Amen.

"Honour your parents", that's what the Bible says. But at the moment I just can't stand them. Why can't they understand how I feel and appreciate my point of view? If only they would stop getting at me. But Lord, you ask me to love them no matter what they're like. It seems you're my only hope of doing that at the moment! Help me to make the effort to understand their way of thinking and to be patient. And help me to control my big mouth, because so often I say things I really don't mean and I start shouting. Amen.

Lord Jesus, I come to you in forgiveness for not being obedient to my parents. It's really hard not to fly off the handle when my parents stop me from doing things. Help me to honour my Mother and Father, and by your Spirit unite us in family love so that we can work things out peacefully. Amen.

Dear Lord, help me to realize that when I argue with my parents, they are only trying to help. Give me consideration for them, and give them wisdom and knowledge to do what is best for me. Amen.

II

For when someone lets you down

DEAR GOD, I know you are my best friend and that you will never let me down. You're always there when I need someone to talk to. But why aren't my friends the same? They sometimes won't talk and sometimes I feel they don't respect my belief in you. All I ask is that they may find friendship and understanding through you. Also, please forgive us all for the wrong things we do. Amen.

Heavenly Father, you know that I have been let down. Lord, help me overcome my feeling of despair and to try to continue with my life as normal. Father, I thank you that you never let me down and that I can always come to you in times of trouble. I pray that my trust will be fully in you during this difficult time. In Jesus' name. Amen.

When someone lets you down you tend to forget that God is there. You sulk and you think you are on your own. Dear Lord, help us not to sulk but to turn to you when things go wrong. Amen.

Dear Lord, help me to be strong. I've been let down by my friend. Let me try and forgive them and not do the same back through spite. Help us to keep our friendship even if we let one another down. Amen.

Dear God, thank you for being my friend. Please help me to understand that other people aren't as perfect as you and can't always be what I expect them to be. Please help me to be a friend to others that they can depend on and trust. Amen.

Dear Father, help me to forgive other people when they hurt me and let me say sorry when I'm wrong. Help me to admit my mistakes when I don't get on with friends and parents. Please give me happiness when I'm depressed, company if I'm lonely and peace if I'm angry. Amen.

Dear Father, help! Amen.

Lord, help me to remember that when someone lets me down you will always be with me, and if I do wrong, you will always be ready to welcome me back. Amen.

Dear Lord, I've been let down. I know I should forgive them, but I find it hard as I have been hurt by someone I trust. I know that I also have let people down and I ask that you will forgive me. I ask that you will help me to forgive the people who have let me down so that we can build our trust and friendship with one another. Amen.

Heavenly Father, help us when our friends let us down, may we always remember that *you* will never do that. Amen.

Dear God, I often feel so annoyed and angry when my friends let me down. I feel lonely and unwanted. Why are they ignoring me, what have I done? Lord, it's hard to forgive. But then I remember how many times I ignore you. Yet you are not bitter, Lord, you still love and forgive me. I am always letting you down, Lord, and I know how you must feel deep down, lonely and unwanted. Yet you are always there for me when I need you. Dear Lord, I am sorry for neglecting you, and I pray that you will give me strength to love you more each day. Amen.

Oh Lord, thanks that you never leave us, no matter how hard life gets or how far I may be feeling from you; you are always there by my side. Lord help me to rely on you, and to put my trust in your steadfast love. You alone will never let me down or desert me in times of trouble. But Lord, teach me to forgive those human friends who fail me when I need them most. Lord, don't let me grow bitter or resentful but renew our love and deepen our friendship. Lord, thanks for your unfailing love for me. Amen.

Part Three

SUFFERING

12

For those suffering with AIDS

LORD, HELP ALL those suffering with AIDS. Help their families to come to terms with what has happened and not to judge them. Help them to live their lives to the full for however long they have left. Give them strength as they have to face the world and show them that your love never fails. Amen.

Jesus, you wouldn't be afraid to touch or love someone with AIDS. You'd invite them to your home and eat with them. You would not judge them if they had sinned. Help me not to judge, help me not to feel scared, help me not to feel helpless. Give me strength to open my arms, my church, my home and my love to anyone who needs it. Help me to be like you. Amen.

Heavenly Father, we pray for those people who are suffering with AIDS. Make them strong and give them courage to carry on. We ask you, Father, that like other diseases, a cure will be found. Help those who suffer to tell others about the danger of this disease. We also pray for the families and friends in their times of sorrow and grief, that they will be able to comfort those who are dying. Support them in their hour of need. Amen.

Dear Lord, throughout the world there are many people who suffer from AIDS and the HIV virus. Often they have caught the disease through no fault of their own and are left weak and ill for the rest of their shortened lives. We pray that a cure is found for this horrific illness and that the suffering of many will soon end. For this we pray with all our hearts. Amen.

Heavenly Father, we pray for all the people in the world suffering from AIDS. We ask that you will give them courage and determination to cope with the disease. We also ask that you will comfort the families of all victims. Amen.

Lord, there are many things that people fear in our world, famine, war, poverty, homelessness – the list seems endless. But these things have all been around for many years and in some ways we understand them. But now we have a new fear which we cannot cope with and do not fully understand – AIDS. People who have AIDS do not have the support of knowing that the problem has been medically treated before. They must feel alone and insecure. Help them to realize that you are always there for them and that you always care – and that we do as well. Amen.

Lord, we pray for those suffering with the HIV virus and for those living around them, be they friends or family. We pray that they will have the help and support they need in times of hardship and illness. We pray for all the doctors and nurses who help with the care of those with this illness and we pray for a speedy cure. Amen.

Lord, please help those people with AIDS or who are HIV positive. Help them in their pain and suffering, and let them know that they are not alone in their grief. Please help ease the pain that their families are going through. Teach those who are ignorant about the disease that they need to give their love and not treat sufferers "like lepers". Help us to learn more about AIDS so that we can find a cure soon and so put hope into the lives of those who suffer. Amen.

Lord God, you love us with a love that knows no limits. But we understand life only in part. In our pain, our anger and our fear, may we still find your love, for you are the only rock we can cling to that will not let us down. Amen.

13

For those with cancer

FATHER, PLEASE HELP all those in our world suffering with cancer. Sadly there are thousands today who are in pain due to this disease. Please give them help and love throughout their illness, and for those who will never recover please give them faith and trust in you. Amen.

Lord, please help all those people fighting against cancer. We all know that it is a terrible disease. Please help them never to give up. Amen.

Lord, we pray for those who have cancer and who worry about what might happen to them. We ask that you will calm their fears and let them know that you know their future and will always be with them. We ask this in your name. Amen.

Dear Lord Jesus, we pray for all those who suffer from incurable diseases. You know what they are going through as you experienced such pain on the cross. Help them to remember that you love them, since they may doubt your love for them, and fill them with your Holy Spirit and never-ending love. Amen.

Dear God, you show love in funny ways, sometimes taking the ones we love the most. Cancer – it's a horrid word, but many people have to cope with its consequences. Help us to deal with the pain and hurt that it causes, because it is at times like these that we need you most. Give us the strength to help others affected by it, and give us the right words and actions with which to comfort them. We need your help, God. Amen.

Lord, can you please give strength to those who are fighting against cancer. Help doctors to find a cure so that people do not have to suffer. Amen.

Dear Lord, we pray for all the people who are suffering from cancer, whether it is curable or incurable. Help them to live a good life during their ordeal, and if it is curable to recover completely. If they are going to die, please let them die peacefully, and look after them in heaven. Amen.

14

For victims of racism

FATHER, WE PRAY for the victims of racism, we pray that you will give them the strength to carry on their lives despite the discrimination. Lord, we also pray that the people who commit acts of discrimination will see sense and abandon their ignorance. Lord, in your name we pray. Amen.

Dear God, please help those people who are suffering from the emotional and physical grief and violence of racism. Please help them forgive the narrow-minded people foolish enough to make remarks about another person in a different race or religion. Amen.

Dear Lord, please help all those in the world who through no fault of their own are subject to discrimination, whether it be racial, social or any other kind. Give them the strength to rise above it, and let them know that you love everyone and hold no one better than others. Amen.

Dear Lord, please help all those who are the victims of racism, and those who cannot accept people of different cultures in their communities. We pray that you will help and guide them to accept everyone, of whatever colour or creed. Amen.

Lord our Father, we are all your children, no matter what colour, race or nationality. May racism become a thing of the past, so that we can all live in harmony. We pray for those who are victims of racism of any kind; and please help those who are racist to see the light of your love. Amen.

Dear God, help us to understand that people are all the same, and that race and skin colour are irrelevant. Help us to see through the outer person and to look deep inside to discover our friend's true character. Amen.

Dear Lord, you made everyone as equals, so help us to accept everyone as our friend, whether they are black or white, disabled or homeless. So Lord, teach us to love one another and to live together in peace and harmony. Amen.

Jesus loves the little children, all the children of the world, red and yellow, black and white, they are all precious is his sight. Jesus loves the little children of the world. Amen.

Heavenly Father, please help us to live in racial harmony, not caring what the colour of a person's skin is but looking to the person inside, seeing only their good points and forgiving them for their bad. Amen.

Lord, help us not to see colour and creed, not to think black or white, race or religion. Let us live in harmony and peace. All are equal in your eyes, and surely they should be in ours too. Amen.

Dear Lord, please help those victims of racism who are bullied because of the colour of their skin, who are picked on because they have different traditions. Help us to remember it doesn't matter what anyone looks like. You love us whatever colour we are. Help us to be like you. Amen.

15

For those coping with the death of a relative or friend

DEAR LORD, WHEN we are trying to cope with the loss of a loved one please give us strength to see it through and to realize that they have passed into your hands, to a much better and happier place. Fill us with your peace over this difficult period of time. Amen.

Dear Lord, it's difficult to cope when someone you love dies. It doesn't seem fair, we want to blame you, even though we know it's not your fault. They may no longer be in pain, but those of us left behind hurt deep inside. Though they may have entered an existence even more beautiful than life, the world seems dark and pointless to those who remain. So I ask you to help all those who cry for those they've loved and lost, so that they may continue to praise you and not lose faith. Amen.

Dear Lord, please help those who have lost a friend or member of their family. Let them remember that however sad they may feel, you will always be there to love and care for them. Amen.

Dear Lord, give us strength in coping with death, the death of someone close to us. Give us confidence in you to know that you are looking after our loved ones. Thank you, Lord. Amen.

Dear Lord Jesus, when you lose a close friend it seems so hard to accept. It's like it never happened, just some horrible nightmare. Oh God, so many questions. Why, what's the point? Why did you take away someone I love, someone so young who never even had a chance to live? When something like this happens it's so easy to become bitter and twisted. Life can become really hopeless. Why have you done this to me, why have you made so many people suffer? Please Lord Jesus, it's so easy to lose hope. Please use this situation and make it meaningful, so that it does not become just another dark area inside, something too painful and too difficult to face. Please use this situation so that their death is meaningful. Oh God, help me to find a purpose so that my life can become real, meaningful and worth living. Amen.

Dear God, help those who are grieving for the loss of a loved one or friend. Be with them at this time and let them know that they have gone to a better place. Amen.

Dear Lord, please help those who have lost someone close to them, and help them understand that their spirit lives on as strong as ever. Amen.

Dear Father God, when a friend or relative is dying they are scared of not knowing what tomorrow holds and where they are going. Please help them and us to realize that they are leaving this world and going into your loving gentle caring hands. Please help those who grieve to grieve less, and those who weep to weep less, and those who don't understand why to understand more. Amen.

16

For those who are outcasts in society

LORD, SOMETIMES WE feel left out and ignored by our friends after some silly quarrel, and we feel hurt and alone. Help us to remember those who feel left out every day, left out by their friends, rejected by society, those for whom luck never seems to come their way. We thank you for the security of our homes and families, and we lift up to you those who this night will not have a roof over their heads and somewhere to go home to. We remember them in the name of your son who was rejected by his people and often felt an outcast of society. Amen.

Father God, help all those who are rejected or outcast from our society, whether it is because of race, religion or appearance. Help us to accept them and put aside any dislikes or prejudices, and to view everyone in the same light. Amen.

Dear Lord, let us remember the quiet people. The ones who sit in the corner all alone. The ones who have no friends because they are a different colour or because they are strange. Let us remember those people and be kind to them. Amen.

Dear God, fill us with your Holy Spirit so that we may be active people for you in this hurting world. Give us strength so that we may come alongside the down-trodden. Let your love flow through us so that we may comfort the outcasts in our society, and teach us humility so that we may put our arms around the unloved. Amen.

Please Lord, help those who are rejected in society for one reason or another. If people are prejudiced towards them give them strength to cope. Amen.

17
For the sick

LORD, WE PRAY that those who are sick can find healing in your love. Those who are lonely can find friendship in your care. Those who feel lost can return to your knowledge. But most of all, Lord, we pray that those who are sad can find contentment in your presence. In Jesus' name. Amen.

Father, we ask that you will give strength and peace to those who are in any way burdened by physical or emotional pain. Help them in their time of need, give others around them compassion and patience to bear witness to them when they are sharing Christ's pain. Lord, we ask this in Jesus' name. Amen.

Lord, very often we only think and pray for ourselves. Please help us to pray for those less fortunate. We forget that there are those who are sick at home and in hospital. We pray that you will look after them and help us all during difficult times. Amen.

Dear God, help us to give thanks for the people who care for us, the hard-working doctors and nurses who make the world a better place to live in. We thank you for our family and friends who care for us when we are ill. Amen.

Lord, give strength to those who are ill, especially those who are terminally ill and know that they don't have long to live. Let them turn to you for help. Amen.

Dear Lord, we pray for all who are sick and needy, especially those with terminal illnesses. May their sorrow and that of their families be calmed by the knowledge that they will soon enter your eternal kingdom to be with you. Help them through their last days on earth so that they may not suffer. For the love of your only son whose suffering was long. Amen.

Lord, in your great glory and mercy we ask you to help all those who suffer sickness or pain, especially those known to us personally. We ask you to be present with those who are terminally ill. Father give to them all your strength, love and peace of mind. Amen.

Dear God, please help all the sick and needy people in this world, along with the old people whom we tend to forget about. Also the homeless and the people with personal problems at home. Amen.

Lord, help those who are sick, help us to help them to get better and make us care for those who are sick. Even if we are worried about our own health give us strength to pick them up when they are down. Keep all those who are sick in good faith. Amen.

18

For the elderly

LORD, PLEASE HELP us to try and understand the things elderly people are going through. Help us to realize that one day we will all end up elderly like them. Let us treat them as we would wish to be treated when we ourselves get older. Amen.

Dear Lord, please give strength to the lonely people who are feeling helpless and rejected, especially to the elderly who are living on the streets. Amen.

Dear God, I pray for the elderly. I pray that people won't ignore them and that they may all have someone who cares for them and visits them regularly to make sure they are all right. I pray that we will treat them like the valuable part of society that they are. Amen.

Dear Lord, we pray for the elderly and sick in nursing homes and hospitals all over the world. We remember the nurses and doctors, and pray that you may give them strength to do their work. Amen.

Dear Lord, please help the elderly and homeless this winter, both in this country and abroad. Let us remember that as we go tobogganning on the slopes, someone somewhere is too cold even to move, too hungry to think, too lonely to care for life itself. Please Lord, warm their hearts with your love and make us realize how privileged we are. Please Lord, hear our prayer. Amen.

Dear Lord Jesus, please continue to give the elderly the love and affection they need. We ask that they will know that you are with them when they are ill or in hospital. Help the families whose fathers or husbands fought in past wars and give them comfort. Amen.

Dear Lord, please help the elderly members of our society, as they form an important part of it. Put it into our minds that we can help them. Amen.

Dear Father God, we pray for the elderly people in our world, especially for the sick or immobile who find it hard to live an everyday life. We pray that we who are capable people will help them to do what they cannot manage on their own. Amen.

19

For those who are handicapped

LORD HELP US to treat handicapped people like ourselves. Though they face many problems and their lives are restricted, they are the same as us inside. Amen.

Dear Father, we know that you love us all, but sometimes it is hard to remember. Let us try to love everyone around us. Help us especially to love those who have a physical or mental disability. Let our love guide them towards you because in you we all become stronger and more loving servants. Teach those who are blind to the qualities of the handicapped people that they can love them too. Amen.

Dear Lord, help those who are handicapped and find life difficult. Bless and guide all those who look after them. Amen.

Lord, help those who are handicapped, give them the strength to try new things and to help others. Also, Lord, help us not to see people who are handicapped as different, but remind us that they are people too. Amen.

Dear God, help those who are handicapped to cope with their disabilities and encourage people to support them and not turn away. Amen.

Lord God, please help me to look upon myself not as handicapped but different. Help me to overcome the sadness I may feel and to know that you are with me always. Amen.

20

For those with drug and alcohol addiction

DEAR LORD, WE pray for those who are either involved in drugs or who are finding it hard to resist drugs from so-called friends. Please give them strength to say, "No!" Amen.

Lord, help those who take harmful drugs, like cocaine and heroin, to overcome their addiction. Help them to understand the harm it does. Give the younger generation the wisdom to realize that drugs like nicotine have an effect on people later on in life. Please make sure that my family, friends and myself never feel the need to take drugs. Amen.

Lord, please help those who have drug and alcohol problems. Help them to be strong and try to overcome their painful situation. Amen.

Lord, we pray for those who use or are tempted to experiment with drugs. We pray that they may realize the danger of what they are doing. I ask that you give us the strength to help those we know who are on drugs, and that we may resist the temptation to take them ourselves. Amen.

God, give strength to those who abuse alcohol and drugs. Give them strength to see the errors of their ways. Many have become homeless due to their addiction. I know it's hard for them to quit. Make them see all the worry and stress they are causing to their family and friends. Help them come to terms with reality and to see that life can have a deeper meaning. Help the dealers to see how much damage and misery they are causing. For you are the only addiction of peace, love and hope. Amen.

Dear Lord, we pray for the many people in this world who are suffering with the problems of alcohol and drug addiction. Help them to overcome their habit and support them in their hour of need. Amen.

Dear Lord, help me to use my eyes as your eyes Lord, to help those who have drug and alcohol problems and not to dismiss them but to commend them to you.

Help me to have the courage to tell them what they are doing to themselves, and to show them there is a way out. I see my friends around me, Lord, doing things I know will harm them. Give me the courage and opportunity to help them. Help them to face up to their problems and grant them the strength to fight. Amen.

Part Four

THE WORLD

For charity organizations

LORD, WE PRAY for all the charities who give help to the sick and needy. We pray that they may help as many people as possible. We pray for those who run various charities, that it may bring fulfilment into their lives as well as of those who they seek to help. Amen.

Thank you for all the world's charity organizations. Please help them use their money wisely in the work they are doing. Help us to give them all the support they need. Amen.

Lord, please help us to give to charities, and not just because we feel guilty about it. Help us to give because we want to. Help us not just to give money but our valuable time as well. Help us to help others in need because that too is charity. Amen.

For when the environment is neglected and destroyed

DEAR GOD, THANK you for making the world and all the beautiful things in it. Help the people who want to destroy our world to realize that you love it and created it for us. Amen.

Lord, help us to look after this planet we live on. You created it and we know that you would not want us to neglect or harm our surroundings in any way. Help us to save endangered animals or plants, because we know that you would hate to see them disappear. Help us to look after our world. Amen.

Dear Lord, gradually our society is destroying this beautiful world you have created. Why do we do it Lord? Is it that we are unable to see how lovely the world is? Surely not? Soon all the trees and fields will be no more. Towering buildings, flats, houses, will be the only thing that the eye can see. Help us to prevent this vastness of destruction and to observe the beauty of this world and not to take it for granted. Amen.

Lord, you gave us this world to live in, not to destroy and abuse. Help us to live in harmony with our surroundings and to think next time we drop litter or use harmful chemicals. The world is our home and we must not destroy it. Amen.

Lord, what are we doing? We are destroying your world. We are killing your creatures without reason for fur coats and just for fun. Help us to see what we are doing and mend our ways. Amen.

Father, forgive us for damaging the world you gave us. For burning the trees and poisoning the oceans. Teach us how to care for our environment as you care for us. Amen.

Almighty God, please show people that the earth is for them and that they are destroying a gift to us from you, and that indirectly they are destroying themselves.

Help all mankind to realize that our world is a precious gift and to be treated with care and respect. Amen.

Dear God, thank you for the world which you created for us. Help us to appreciate the living things around us, especially when we take things for granted. I pray that you will help us to protect our environment so that it is always there to remind us of you and what you have done for us. Amen.

Lord, we pray for the environment we live in, the quiet and peaceful countryside or the noisy and busy town. Help us keep these places free of litter and help us stop the people who neglect or destroy our environment. Amen.

Lord, is it right to destroy what you have created? Is it right to tear up the countryside to make way for high rise flats when there are derelict houses just waiting to be lived in? Every single animal and plant has a use in life, why do we ignore and neglect them Lord? This world you have created has everything we need but slowly we are destroying it. Help us realize what we are doing before we get into deep trouble. Amen.

The World

O Lord, you gave us so much beauty in the world in which we live, yet we do not do our part and look after it. We neglect it, we even go so far as to destroy it. Help us, Lord, to take care of all your creation, and forgive us for all the damage that we have done. We pray this in the name of our Lord Jesus Christ. Amen.

23

For our Church and Christian leaders

FATHER IN HEAVEN, we pray for our leaders. Help them to speak out with your love and to be strong in your truth. Give them wisdom and courage. Amen.

Lord, each week you bring us together as a community in your love and fellowship to worship you and to draw us closer to your love. As a fellowship we seek to follow the path you have shown us and to be obedient to your word. Help us, Lord, as we come each week to worship you, to get to know you better. Amen.

Dear Lord, please bless all our religious leaders who follow in the foosteps of the Apostles by drawing people into your holy Church. The General Synod's decision to ordain women priests continues to cause division in your Church. No matter what our views are, Lord, we thank you for the reassurance given by your Holy Spirit that you will remain with us always, even in the deepest sorrow or confusion. Let the ministers of your Church continue to spread the good news to the world and fill them with your love and understanding so that they may continue to serve in your name. Amen

Dear Lord, help the Church to grow in number and in love and help those who go to church not to think it's boring or a waste of time. Amen.

Dear Lord, please help our church and churches all over the world to grow and encourage others to seek you. Help us to understand and accept your word. Give courage to those who are persecuted because of their beliefs and love for you. We ask that your love may rule *all* the earth and that we may live in peace and be ruled by love. We ask this in your name. Amen.

Dear Lord, we thank you for our church. We give thanks especially for all the people involved in the life of our church; for our Vicar and Wardens, for the choir and Readers, for the ladies who clean and arrange the flowers, for Sunday School teachers, youth leaders and sidesmen. We pray that by your grace, all the members of our church will continue to work together to further your Kingdom. In Jesus' name. Amen.

Lord, church didn't go too well today. I thought a church was supposed to be one big family but ours is just a battle between young and old. Lord, help each of us to understand each other. Amen.

Lord, as we pray for the Church all over the world, help us to remember that it is your love that joins us all together. We thank you for the friendly community that the church brings and for all the people who work in the church. We ask you to bless them and all that they do for you, so that your Spirit may guide us all in the right direction towards your love. In Jesus' name we pray. Amen.

Dear God, we pray for all those who are lonely. Please help us to be kind and helpful to them. May they feel wanted and welcome in your church. Thank you, God. Amen.

Dear Father, bring all churches together so that they may be united in your name. Help the congregation both young and old to be guided in worship by you.

Often the young feel unwelcome in the services. Help the older members to encourage the young, so that the Christian life may continue to grow and flourish. We ask this in Jesus' name. Amen.

24

For peace in our world

LORD, GIVE YOUR children peace. Amen.

Dear Lord, help us to live together without war but in peace, and to love each other as you love us. Amen.

Lord, I feel your world isn't working. People from many countries and cultures are trying to prove their power and strength through war and terrorism. Please Lord, bring peace into this world and forgive all those who have caused death and destruction by their actions. Let us join together as one world so that we can share what we have and help others. Amen.

Father, please give those in positions of power the knowledge and strength to resolve problems and conflicts of opinion by peaceful means. Please help people to strive for peace not war, and above all let there be understanding between different peoples and nationalities. Amen.

Dear Lord, please help us to stop fighting and teach us to think and talk things over peacefully, so that we can reach a compromise instead of using weapons. Amen.

Dear Lord, peace is still something quoted by politicians but rarely implemented. Please allow the most fragile area of the world, the Middle East, to achieve peace. Please help dictators around the world to turn to democracy, where individual people count as they do in your eyes. Help peace rule the world. Amen

Grant us, Lord God, the vision of your Kingdom, with forgiveness and new life and the stirring of your Spirit. So that we may share your vision, proclaim your love and change the world, in the name of Christ. Amen.

Dear God, may there be peace in our world and an end to war and fighting. Amen.

Lord, please help us to mend and remake this broken world you gave us. Help our world leaders to make the right decisions. This is the world that your son Jesus died for, so it should be treasured and not destroyed by evil gases and global war. Please help us save our planet. Amen.

25

For our government and world leaders

DEAR LORD, PLEASE be with those who are in positions of authority, both in our country and around the world. Their decisions affect all our lives, so help them to choose the right things to do, so that your name may be honoured. Amen.

Our Father, help us to be more aware of the pressure involved in holding a position of power. It is the easiest thing in the world to look on and criticize. We do not see the full picture or the effort in areas which do not affect us. So we pray for all our leaders. Amen.

Lord God our Father, we ask you to bless our Queen and all the Royal Family. Please inspire the statesmen who meet in council to maintain peace, and to make the world safe from nuclear weapons. We ask that you would guide and direct all who negotiate with foreign rulers to free prisoners and hostages. For Jesus' sake. Amen.

Dear Lord, we pray for our government and world leaders. Please give them wisdom to make the right decisions and determination to execute the right plans, and help them to achieve a peaceful world for us all to live in. We ask this in the name of our Saviour Jesus Christ. Amen.

Dear Lord, please help our government and world leaders to decide what is best for the world of tomorrow. We pray that they will make just and right decisions in your name, Lord. Amen.

Our Father, we thank you for the world we live in, the food we eat and the people we know. We pray for peace between all nations, and that you will guide our leaders so that they can restore harmony into our world. Amen.

Lord, aid our political and spiritual leaders to endeavour to make the right decisions. Give them strength to understand the problems that your children face all over the world. Help them avoid instability, warfare and starvation, and attempt to promote unity throughout the globe. Amen.

Lord, we pray for the world and all its problems. In the world you created there is suffering, violence, poverty and famine. There are endless world disasters and we could not begin to name them all. So we bring our concerns about the world to you and ask that you will give your people strength in their faith to carry on. Instead of hatred and fear, grant us peace and hope. Amen.

Dear God, we pray for peace in our world. Not just the absence of war but good trusting relationships between all nations. Please show our national leaders other ways to end disputes rather than war. Help them to realize that hospitals, schools and food are more important than tanks and missiles. We really want peace. Please help us to know what we can do to promote true peace in our world. Amen.

Part Five

IN THANKS

26

For when you are grateful to God

O GOD! THANK you, thank you, thank you. Amen.

Father, when I talk to you I don't use those long, beautiful and descriptive words. But I know that whatever I have to say and however simply I speak to you, you will listen and understand me. Thanks. Amen.

Lord, thank you for your amazing love for me. You came down to earth and gave your only Son for *me*. I turn away from you continually but you carry on loving me. There is nothing we have ever done or ever will do that makes us deserve your love, and we hardly ever even thank you for it. So Lord, thank you. Amen.

Dear Father, very often we take for granted all the things around us, never considering that all the comforts may one day be taken from us. Through your guidance, Lord, may we be able to pray and help those who are less fortunate than ourselves. May we always remember how much we have and, being grateful, give thanks and praise to you. Amen.

Lord, thank you for dying for us. By the perfect sacrifice of your body and blood, you give us the opportunity to be forgiven and re-united with God. Help us, like the Apostles, to trust and believe in you though we cannot fully comprehend the mystery of this sacrament. Amen.

Dear God, let me realize how grateful I should be for all I have. Let me help others who need support. Amen.

Oh Lord, we are grateful for everything you have given us – the food we eat and the water we drink. Also, thank you for what you have done, are doing and will be doing for us. Amen.

Dear God, I would like to thank you for sending your

Son to this earth to live among us, so that we can identify with you. It's really quite amazing to know that all the problems we have or will ever have you understand because Jesus was human too. It's also great to know that, like Jesus, we can overcome our problems by fully trusting you to help us, not to skip over the problem but to plough through. Father, I ask you to help me to live my life like Jesus did. Give me faith to trust you fully, even when everything around tries to knock me off course. Father, please send your Spirit down on us and help us to let him in, to enable us to be more like Jesus. Amen.

Dear Lord, there are no words that can describe our thanks, for without you we would not exist, we would not be here reading this prayer. Everything is you, what we see, hear and do. Every decision we make is influenced by you. So we thank you again, Lord, for everything; for all that is good and which makes us happy, and all that is bad, which helps us to learn. Amen.

Dear Lord God and heavenly King, we thank and praise you for your love and heartfelt concern for each one of us. So much so that you, King of all Kings, should send your own Son down to us not even as a king but as a baby, a child born in a stable, cold and wet, destined for nothing but a working man's life as a carpenter. But through our cruel world he was crucified on a cross to die as a criminal. Amen.

> Lord, thanks for being with me through trouble and strife,
> being there in my everyday life,
> helping me not to brag and boast,
> being there when I needed you most,
> showing me that you are always there,
> giving me your love and care. Amen.